SpringerBriefs in Criminology

SpringerBriefs in Policing

Series Editor
M. R. Haberfeld, John Jay College of Criminal Justice
City University of New York
New York, NY, USA

SpringerBriefs in Criminology present concise summaries of cutting edge research across the fields of Criminology and Criminal Justice. It publishes small but impactful volumes of between 50-125 pages, with a clearly defined focus. The series covers a broad range of Criminology research from experimental design and methods, to brief reports and regional studies, to policy-related applications.

The scope of the series spans the whole field of Criminology and Criminal Justice, with an aim to be on the leading edge and continue to advance research. The series will be international and cross-disciplinary, including a broad array of topics, including juvenile delinquency, policing, crime prevention, terrorism research, crime and place, quantitative methods, experimental research in criminology, research design and analysis, forensic science, crime prevention, victimology, criminal justice systems, psychology of law, and explanations for criminal behavior.

SpringerBriefs in Criminology will be of interest to a broad range of researchers and practitioners working in Criminology and Criminal Justice Research and in related academic fields such as Sociology, Psychology, Public Health, Economics and Political Science.

SpringerBriefs in Policing presents concise summaries of cutting edge research in Police Science, across the fields of Criminology, Criminal Justice, Psychology, Forensic Science, and Corrections with implications for the study of police and police work. It publishes small but impactful volumes of between 50-125 pages, with a clearly defined focus. The series covers a broad range of Policing research: from experimental design and methods, to brief reports and regional case studies, to policy-related applications. The scope of the series spans the subfield of Policing, with an aim to be on the leading edge and continue to advance research. The series is international and cross-disciplinary, including a broad array of topics. The main goal of the series is to present innovations in Policing, in order to further the field as a research and evidence-based profession rather than a vocational occupation. It will showcase how Policing confronts problems and challenges that transcend cultures and borders and can be addressed from a global rather than local perspective. SpringerBriefs in Policing is aimed at a broad range of researchers and practitioners working in Criminology and Criminal Justice Research and in related academic fields such as Public Policy, Sociology, Psychology, Public Health, Economics, Policy Analysis, Terrorism and Political Science.

Lorna Ferguson • Laura Huey

Police Search and Rescue Response to Lost and Missing Persons

Springer

Lorna Ferguson
Department of Sociology
University of Western Ontario
London, ON, Canada

Laura Huey
Department of Sociology
University of Western Ontario
London, ON, Canada

ISSN 2192-8533 ISSN 2192-8541 (electronic)
SpringerBriefs in Criminology
ISSN 2194-6213 ISSN 2194-6221 (electronic)
SpringerBriefs in Policing
ISBN 978-3-031-44076-2 ISBN 978-3-031-44077-9 (eBook)
https://doi.org/10.1007/978-3-031-44077-9

This Springer imprint is published by the registered company Springer Nature Switzerland AG
The registered company address is: Gewerbestrasse 11, 6330 Cham, Switzerland

Paper in this product is recyclable.

To the lost and missing persons; the families and loved ones of the missing; the police involved in missing persons and SAR work; the SAR partners and volunteers across Canada; and all other non-police SAR groups—this book is dedicated to you. We recognize and hold space for the stories of the lost and missing in these chapters, and their families and loved ones who experienced these incidents.

Acknowledgments

Thank you to all police and non-police SAR personnel who devote themselves to this work and locating and recovering thousands of lost and missing persons year after year.

Thank you especially to the police personnel who were involved in any part of this book, including interviews, online surveys, collaboration to share data, and providing feedback.

The research contained in this book was supported by funding from the Vanier Canada Graduate Scholarships, Social Science and Humanities (SSHRC).

Contents

About the Authors

Lorna Ferguson Vanier Scholar Lorna Ferguson is a PhD(c) at the University of Western Ontario and is the Founder of the Missing Persons Research Hub. She is a criminologist who has dedicated over nine years to studying crime and criminal justice and working in this field. Overall, her research interests pertain to the sociology of work with respect to policing and developing evidence-based approaches to policing and crime prevention, including the study of issues related to crime concentration, police data, and cybercrime. Her research specialization is police responses to missing persons cases. This research aims to fill in knowledge gaps on the police role and function and, generally, police work in this area. It focuses on investigating "what works," "what doesn't work," and "what we still don't know" in terms of most effectively and efficiently searching for and investigating missing persons. She has educated, trained, and collaborated and partnered with over 40 police services and several individual police officers across Canada to enhance police practices and policies and police officer knowledge on missing persons. Lorna's research has also been published in numerous peer-reviewed journals in her field and has been the subject of many local, national, and international presentations. Her most recent research has appeared in *Criminology & Criminal Justice*, *Crime and Delinquency*, *Policing & Society*, *Policing: A Journal of Policy and Practice*, *Policing: An International Journal*, and *Deviant Behavior*.

Laura Huey Dr. Laura Huey is Professor of Sociology at the University of Western Ontario, Editor of Police Practice & Research, Chair of the Working Group on Mental Health and Policing of the Royal Society of Canada, Vice-Chair of the American Society of Criminologists' Division of Policing, and the former Executive Director of the Canadian Society of Evidence-Based Policing. She is also a member of the College of New Scholars, Artists, and Scientists of the Royal Society of Canada, the Editor in Chief of Police Practice and Research, and a Senior Research Fellow with the US National Police Foundation.

Dr. Huey's work in the field of crime and security is primarily focused on policing (frontline and criminal investigation), victimization, terrorism, and cybersecurity. Her research has appeared in the *British Journal of Sociology*, the *British*

Journal of Criminology, *Sociological Review*, *Society & Mental Health*, *Theoretical Criminology*, *Criminology and Criminal Justice*, the *Journal of Interpersonal Violence*, and various other international journals. She has authored several books on policing and the provision of security. She is also an International Advisory Editor for *Theoretical Criminology* and on the editorial advisory boards of *Policing: A Journal of Policy and Practice* and the *Canadian Journal of Criminology and Criminal Justice*.

Abbreviations

ATM	Automated Teller Machine
ATV	All-Terrain Vehicle
BC	British Columbia
BLE	Bluetooth Low Energy
CAD	Computer Aided Dispatch
CAF	Canadian Armed Forces
CAMSAR	Canadian Aeronautical and Maritime Search and Rescue Manual
CASAR	Canadian Association of Search and Rescue
CASARA	Civil Air Search and Rescue Association
CCIMA	Canadian Centre for Information on Missing Adults
CCGA	Canadian Coast Guard Auxiliary
CCTV	Closed-Circuit Television
CCU	Cold Case Unit
CPIC	Canadian Police Information Centre
ECD	Emergency Call-Takers and Dispatchers
EMBC	Emergency Management British Columbia
FLIR	Forward-Looking Infrared
GNSS	Global Navigation Satellite System
GPS	Global Positioning System
GSAR	Ground Search and Rescue
GSM	Global System for Mobile Communications
IAMSAR	International Aeronautical and Maritime Search and Rescue Manual
ICAO	International Civil Aviation Organization
ICS	Incident Command System
IMO	International Maritime Organization
IO	Investigating Officer
IPP	Initial Planning Point
JRCC	Joint Rescue Coordination Centre
K9	Canine
LE Analyst	Law Enforcement Analyst
LKP	Last Known Place

MDT	Mobile Device Terminal
MibSAR	Michigan Backcountry Search and Rescue
NCMPUR	National Centre for Missing Persons and Unidentified Remains
NSP	National Search and Rescue Program
NSRO	National Search and Rescue Organization
NSRS	National Search and Rescue Secretariat
OPP	Ontario Provincial Police
OSARVA	Ontario Search and Rescue Volunteer Association
PDS	Police Dog Services
PLK	Place Last Known
PLS	Place Last Seen
POA	Probability of Area
POD	Probability of Detection
POU	Public Order Unit
QV7	QuoVadis-7
QVX	QuoVadis-X
RCMP	Royal Canadian Mounted Police
RF	Radio Frequency
RMS	Record Management System
ROV	Remote Operated Vehicle
RPAS	Remote Piloted Aircraft Systems
SAR	Search and Rescue
SAR Docs	Search and Rescue Documents
SARVAC	Search and Rescue Volunteer Association of Canada
SOLAS	International Convention for the Safety of Life at Sea
UAV	Unmanned Aerial Vehicle
US	United States
VPR	Vulnerable Persons Registry

Chapter 1
Introduction to Search and Rescue in Canada

1.1 Where Do the Police Fit?

Makkovik, Labrador (January 2012) The Canadian Shield is a tough, physical landscape, combining rocky outcrops and sparse terrain with vast forest spaces formed by the retreat of massive glaciers. Long home to the Inuit, Innu, and other peoples, its harsh terrain is dotted with smaller communities, many of which subsist on mining and logging. Located across much of eastern Canada's northern reaches, the Shield forms part of the country's sub-Arctic territory, with temperatures often hovering around −18° Celsius in the winter.

On one such bitterly cold day in January, Rodney and Natalie Winters' 14-year-old son, Burton Winters, failed to return home. Growing increasingly concerned, and with weather conditions worsening, they contacted family and friends. Unable to locate Burton, the Royal Canadian Mounted Police (RCMP) were notified, and search and rescue (SAR) personnel were dispatched to look for him. The SAR operation faced multiple resource and weather challenges over the course of the first three days. On the fourth day, tragically, they found Burton frozen to death on sea ice after a snowmobile accident left him stranded.

This story highlights the importance of SAR operations, particularly in critical scenarios where missing individuals are exposed to challenging conditions and thus are at risk of serious harm. In this case, a series of issues related to limited resources, possible miscommunication between agencies, and severe weather conditions resulted in a loss of life (Atter, 2021). Fortunately, of the some 70,000 plus police CPIC[1] reports of missing persons occurring in Canada each year, the overwhelming

[1] CPIC is the Canadian Police Information Centre, which provides access to a repository of various police reports. It is a national information-sharing system operated by the RCMP on behalf of law enforcement in Canada.

L. Ferguson, L. Huey, *Police Search and Rescue Response to Lost and Missing Persons*, SpringerBriefs in Criminology,
https://doi.org/10.1007/978-3-031-44077-9_1

majority are located or return alive and well (Canada's Missing, 2022). Most missing persons cases—around 60%—are also resolved within 24 hours (Canada's Missing, 2022). However, just as with Burton, there are also those situations in which individuals do not and are uniquely vulnerable, because of weather conditions, terrain, age, physical health, mental health, and other issues.

Canada has one of the world's biggest and most challenging areas for SAR, with more than 243,042 kilometers of coastline, three million lakes, three oceans, and the St. Lawrence River system (Public Safety Canada, 2023). The nation's environment adds complexity to these operations. The more north you go, the colder, rockier, snowier, and overall more inhospitable it becomes. Burton's case shows how SAR can be challenging in these areas as the ice conditions impacted access and searching by ground and air (Atter, 2021; Igloliorte, 2021a). Southern Canada is generally the most livable, but great geographic diversity exists in the south, from dense green valleys to dry, sandy deserts to massive metropolitan areas near large bodies of water. Given Canada's immense size, the often austere terrain, and diverse weather conditions, SAR has been constructed as a shared responsibility and is multi-jurisdictional, including government, military, volunteer, and industry groups, who work together to provide these services (Government of Canada, 2018a). As the saying goes, it takes a village to find missing persons in Canada.

Where do the police fit into this? Police are the first to be called upon to respond to missing persons incidents in each agency's particular region of a province or territory. Police bear the primary responsibility for these reports, playing a critical part in the location and resolution of missing persons cases (Denver et al., 2007; Ferguson et al., 2021; Pfeifer, 2006). However, this policing area has yet to generate much attention from academic researchers, the media, and the public, especially regarding processes and activities. A recent study found no previously published, peer-reviewed, empirical research on police SAR teams and their work in Canada (Ferguson et al., 2021). Instead, the focus is on non-police work or SAR operations in large-scale crises and natural disasters (Ferguson et al., 2021; see the Missing Persons Research Hub research database). These insights are, of course, immensely valuable for the field more broadly, but the policing domain still remains largely unaccounted for in the literature. This timely book offers a detailed examination of the routine practices of police SAR personnel or their work "in the most literal sense of the term" (Bittner, 1990, p. 4).

A collection of data has been analyzed and presented in this volume: hundreds of qualitative interviews and online surveys with police personnel across Canada and thousands of different types of missing persons records from multiple police services (see Appendix). Pooling these data offers a comprehensive picture of police SAR, from police perceptions and experiences to missing persons and case incident information to SAR procedures, practices, and policies. It investigates this largely unexplored occupational setting through the policing lens to add to public and scholarly understanding of this type of work and, with this, extends the range of sites of occupational research.

1.2 Defining Lost and Missing Persons

Two key terms used throughout this book are *missing persons* and *lost persons*. In policing, lost and missing people are categorized under the umbrella term of "missing persons" for service calls, response, reporting, and data purposes. Police are concerned with whether the case requires SAR action, not necessarily whether they are lost versus missing. However, these distinctions can play a part in their work, as we discuss in later chapters. For parsimony, we refer to these cases in combination as "missing persons," but definitions and differences are offered below for context.

1.2.1 Missing Persons

Missing persons is a broad concept used to capture a range of disappearances. Various definitions of who and what incidents should be considered a missing person have been used across multiple contexts, such as in the health versus social sector, academic disciplines including criminology versus psychology, and professionally within police and non-police SAR groups. Across Canada, the definition employed within every province and territory varies (Kiepal et al., 2012; Ferguson et al., 2021). Even between each police organization, there are differences. One reason for this is that provincial and territorial governments form local policing regulations and policies in Canada (Huey, 2019), so Canada does not have national policing standards. This means there are generally no national, standardized guidelines or frameworks to offer consistency in missing persons' practice and policy; every province and territory can (and does) do something different. Other reasons are at play, too, like missing persons as a phenomenon is complex and nuanced, requiring case-by-case responses. For this book, we rely on the definition established by the National Centre for Missing Persons and Unidentified Remains (NCMPUR):[2] "Anyone reported to police or by police as someone whose whereabouts are unknown, whatever the circumstances of their disappearance, and they are considered missing until located" (Canada's Missing, 2014).

Missing persons legislation cropping up for policing has impacted the description of a missing person. Multiple regions across Canada have enacted a *Missing Persons Act* or similar to establish provisions for improving police missing persons investigations. While the Acts are comparable, slight differences exist across regions. For example, some Acts specify particular criteria surrounding safety and welfare fears in their description of a missing person (age, capabilities, and disappearance circumstances), while others involve more of a catch-all definition (see British Columbia, 2014 versus Ontario, 2018). There has been some discussion that catch-all definitions and criteria have increased the number of missing persons reports police handle (Ferguson, 2022), but this is inconclusive presently.

[2]The NCMPUR is Canada's national center operated by the RCMP (Canada's Missing, 2014).

1.2.2 Lost Persons

Lost persons is sometimes distinguished from *missing persons* conceptually (i.e., not in practice or policy) as the latter are thought to choose to disappear and do not wish to be found (Foo, 2012). Conversely, Foo (2012) notes that a lost person is "a person who is temporarily disorientated [sic] and would wish to be found, e.g., someone who has gone walking and does not know where they are (and how to return)" (p. 173). Ontario Provincial Police (OPP) (2019) missing persons policy emphasizes that "A lost person is always missing, but a missing person is not always lost. Every missing person shall be considered as lost until proven otherwise." A lost person is also deemed unable to identify or orient themselves to known locations and has no effective means or method for reorientation (Hill, 1998; Hashimoto et al., 2022). The inability to find their bearings often results in lost persons engaging in several behaviors that are notable considerations for SAR. For instance, a hiker may know to rely on aids such as roads and trails or follow water when lost; thus, concentrating SAR activities along such paths increases the chances of finding lost hikers.

Another example is *wanderers*. Wandering behavior can be either aimless or purposeful, typically involving eloping, eloping attempts, and getting lost, sometimes without the orientation to time and place (Petonito et al., 2013; Neubauer et al., 2018). Wandering is linked to age-related cognitive disorders like Alzheimer's and dementia (Neubauer et al., 2018). These persons tend to travel in one direction until they are stopped or get stuck and cannot go any further (Koester, 2008; Ferguson et al., 2021). Focusing on high-hazard areas and barriers near the place the person was last seen, such as ravines and rivers, and following paths that they could freely travel are tactics for likely finding wanderers (Koester, 2008; Foo, 2012; Hashimoto et al., 2022).

SAR response is often tailored to different *lost person behaviors* (Cornell & Hill, 2005; Koester, 2008; Heth & Cornell, 2005). Examining lost person behavior is a prominent area of the research literature, including *Lost Person Behaviour* by Kenneth Hill (1998) and *Lost Person Behavior* by Robert J. Koester (2008).

1.3 Search and Rescue in Canada

1.3.1 Defining Search and Rescue

SAR can involve locating or recovering any person or their remains, who became missing, lost, injured, or killed (Iglolioirte, 2021b; Government of Canada, 2018a). This work is not limited to missing persons; SAR is vital in many disasters and emergencies, like mudslides, building collapses, and forest fires (Public Safety Canada, 2021b). The terms *search and rescue* denote two separate but interconnected functions. *Searching* is a systematic search effort to locate people in emergency situations where they are missing, lost, stranded, or trapped, and their location is unknown. *Rescuing* entails saving or extracting people from emergencies where their location is known, but they need to be removed from danger and returned to safety. Many rescues require no searching, and many searches require no rescuing (Government of Canada, 1996).

1.3.2 Canada's Search and Rescue System

Canada's SAR system has federal, provincial and territorial, and local facilities to meet the unique needs of the landscape and populace. It comprises a complex mosaic of responsibilities and jurisdictions with resources, expertise, and specialized skills in a range of national and local bodies, public service agents, and groups and organizations (Government of Canada, 2013b). Because of this, SAR programs, tools and technologies, and personnel vary geographically per jurisdictional needs and available resources (Igloliorte, 2021b).

Public Safety Canada is a vital federal government service that coordinates the National Search and Rescue Program (NSP) and works to develop national SAR guidelines and advance federal policy. NSP is a cross-government and Canada-wide program for coordination and cooperation; it works directly with federal, provincial and territorial, and local partners and volunteer groups in SAR operations. The responsibility for this program rests with the Minister of National Defense, established as the Lead Minister and delegated the authority, duty, and accountability for the NSP (Igloliorte, 2021b; Public Safety Canada, 2021a). The National Search and Rescue Secretariat (NSRS) was instituted to provide direct, independent support to the Lead Minister, including responsibility and accountability for the conduct of the NSP. Since 2016, the NSRS has also been under the authority of Public Safety Canada (Igloliorte, 2021b).

Other federal responsibilities include the Meteorological Service of Canada, which, under the Department of Environment Canada, assists with environmental considerations such as weather forecasts and warnings of environmental hazards that may impact SAR missions. Next is the Canadian Armed Forces (CAF) in the Department of National Defense. The CAF primarily provides SAR air services (Government of Canada, 2018a; National Defence, 2018). The CAF also helps with ground search and rescue (GSAR) operations (e.g., SAR on land or in adjacent waters), but only when called upon by a law enforcement agency with jurisdictional authority. As a part of the Department of Fisheries and Oceans, the Canadian Coast Guard is federally responsible for coordinating the response to maritime SAR incidents and delivering maritime response resources (National Defence, 2018). Parks Canada leads GSAR and provides resources for national reserves and parks, and Transport Canada offers aviation support. The Canadian Rangers, a subcomponent of the Canadian Army Reserve, also assist with GSAR on an ad hoc basis but mainly in sparsely populated areas of Canada (Government of Canada, 2018a; National Defence, 2018). All federal partners are organized by Joint Rescue Coordination

Centres (JRCCs) in Victoria, Trenton, and Halifax that coordinate the federal response in each region of jurisdiction for all of Canada (Government of Canada, 2013b; Igloliorte, 2021b).

Volunteer groups are a part of the federal and provincial and territorial domains. While SAR remains the task of the police service of jurisdiction, in most areas, local volunteer teams have been established with expertise in tracking, canine search, equestrian search, dive recovery, aquatic rescue, mountain rescue, cave rescue, and other specializations (Igloliorte, 2021b). For aeronautics, the Civil Air Search and Rescue Association (CASARA) voluntarily delivers air SAR support services to the CAF in downed aircraft, as well as training on search techniques and procedures (CASARA, 2022). The volunteers of the Canadian Coast Guard Auxiliary (CCGA) (2022) are dedicated to providing SAR support on federal waterways involving persons or vessels. Another is the Search and Rescue Volunteer Association of Canada (SARVAC) that assists police with land and inland water operations (SARVAC, 2017). Volunteer groups are on standby 24 hours a day, seven days a week, to assist in SAR missions (Public Safety Canada, 2021c).

Lastly, local governments have delegated the authority for GSAR operations to federal, provincial, and municipal police organizations (Government of Canada, 2018a). However, only some services have in-agency SAR teams or personnel. Others have police officers trained and scattered throughout the organization to be deployed as needed and delegate selected tasks to external partners and groups. Some agencies do not engage in this work, aside from initiating SAR response by involving external groups and then maintaining oversight of the cases (Ferguson & Gaub, 2021). Police involvement depends upon resources, agency size, environmental considerations, and available support. To illustrate, the public inquiry on the Burton case remarked that police in smaller Canadian communities "lack the human resources, the specialized knowledge, and often the specialized equipment to actually conduct intensive ground searches for missing persons. Thus, while they always maintain overall authority over an operation, they generally task much of the actual searching to volunteers" (Igloliorte, 2021a, p. 11).

1.3.3 Global Search and Rescue System

There is also a global system connected to SAR in Canada. The International Civil Aviation Organization (ICAO) and the International Maritime Organization (IMO) globally coordinate member countries' efforts to provide SAR services (Government of Canada, 2023a, 2023b). The general goals of the ICAO and IMO are to provide a system available to assist those in need of SAR wherever people travel, regardless of nationality or circumstance (Cooper, 2005). As a part of these objectives, the ICAO and IMO produced the *International Aeronautical and Maritime Search and Rescue (IAMSAR) Manual*. This supplies a three-volume international approach to organizing SAR operations (International Maritime Organization, 2019). Supplementing this is a version adapted for Canada: *Canadian Aeronautical and Maritime Search and Rescue (CAMSAR) Manual* (RCMSAR, 2014). Another global resource is COSPAS-SARSAT, the network of ground stations, mission control centers, satellites, and over 200 SAR rescue coordination centers and points of contact worldwide. This is used to detect; locate; and deploy aircraft, ship, or maritime; or individual distress and emergency alerts around the world (Public Safety Canada, 2023).

There are also international conventions or written agreements establishing rules between countries. These include, but are not limited to, the International Convention for the Safety of Life at Sea (SOLAS), the International Convention on Maritime Search and Rescue, and the Convention on International Aviation (Government of Canada, 2013a; Government of Canada, 2018b; Government of Canada, n.d.; Cooper, 2005). Such agreements include guidelines for countries to provide maritime and aeronautical SAR cooperation and services for their territories and territorial seas (Cooper, 2005). Together, Canada's SAR system is involved in a broader network of organizations, tools, and personnel that cooperate to locate missing persons worldwide.

1.4 The Data

To better understand the police SAR response to missing persons cases in Canada, five complementary data sources are employed in this book: qualitative interviews; online surveys; police Computer-Aided Dispatch (CAD) records; missing persons reports from police Record Management Systems (RMS); and risk, search evaluation, and search questionnaire data. These data contain country-wide information with national, provincial, and territorial details. Thus, a broad account of police SAR in Canada specific to the police role and function, work and operations, and knowledge and expertise is presented. More information on all data can be found in the ***Appendix***, but a brief account is supplied here.

This book draws upon the analysis of findings from 221 qualitative interviews and online surveys with police officers across Canada who have professional experience in SAR work. These data involve police personnel who are Searchers, Search Managers, Search Coordinators, Incident Commanders, Public Order Unit personnel, and others. The interviews and online surveys capture police perceptions and experiences of the roles and functions, types of cases, protocols for handling cases, challenges, issues, training, operations, technologies, tools, and more. These data contribute a panoptic look at this work from the policing perspective.

Interview and online survey data are joined with various police datasets (CAD; RMS; and Risk, search evaluation, and search questionnaire data) spanning multiple years (2014–2019) and containing 22,373 missing persons files. CAD and RMS data provide task, response, and other information on missing persons cases as they progress from initiation to response. CAD data detail the call-for-service correspondence between the reportee and police call-taker, dispatch, and Initial Responding Officer. RMS data feature synopses of SAR operations, any subsequent follow-up actions such as investigations, and case outcomes and closures. CAD data, therefore, provide the details at the earliest onset of the investigation, and RMS data supply all subsequent information following the initial response until the case is concluded (e.g., located, returned, body or remains found). Combined, CAD and RMS data offer organizational and operational insights related to police SAR practices, policies, and processes; these supply documented records of how police responded to missing persons events. Risk, search evaluation, and search questionnaire data detail the urgency assessment and risk factor information from the life of over 8,000 missing persons reports. These data offer information on police case prioritization and risk assessment procedures for missing persons.

Lastly, to collect the materials used in this book to provide context for understanding SAR and police SAR in Canada, we read everything we could find on the subject—everything from news articles, Public Safety Canada and other Government publications, grey literature like theses and policy briefs, presentations, magazine articles, and academic literature. We conducted searches for additional materials using the Google search engine and our institutional library connected to around 800 databases.

After over six years of gathering and analyzing data and related materials for a larger project on missing persons and the police work that goes into resolving these cases, this book is the outcome.

1.5 Chapter "Map"

The chapters explore central questions such as "What does the police SAR response look like? What types of processes are a part of this police work? Who is involved at each stage of the response to missing persons reports? What are the issues, challenges, and strengths of this work? What more can and needs to be done, and how?" Answering such questions by presenting a detailed picture of police SAR as a part of Canada's partnered response is the ultimate goal of this book.

Chapter 2 begins by exploring the organization of police SAR. It offers background context on police personnel involved in this work and their diverse roles and responsibilities. It explains the division of labor, the structure and chain of command, and the various roles and functions pertaining to police SAR members and teams. Chapter 2 then situates this work within the broader police hierarchy, explaining the web of different police units connected to this work to uncover how these personnel and their duties are scattered and embedded in the policing system.

Chapter 3 documents the beginning of police involvement in these cases, with a missing person incident occurring and a citizen contacting the police. It highlights the call-taker's initiation of a missing persons report and alerting the police for response. It then traces the report through the police system at this early stage, delving into the primary response activities, including information-gathering and risk/priority assessment. This chapter is dedicated to discovering the chain of events that launch a police SAR response.

Chapters 4 and 5 are two parts dedicated to delineating the work of police SAR. Particularly, Chap. 4 (Part I) dives into what follows the decision to launch a police SAR response, looking at the various tasks, resources, and duties. It concentrates on what is known as "ground pounding" and the range of police response activities. This chapter also explains lost persons behavior and how the types of cases can impact the work of police SAR. Then, Chap. 5 (Part II) identifies the tools, technologies, and other resources used in police SAR related to the various tasks and responses. Tools and technologies discussed include drones, helicopters, K9 Searchers, and infrared imaging, among others. It also describes other activities relevant to the operation, including police investigations and communication with families and loved ones of the missing.

Chapter 6 focuses on the events following the police SAR response. It first explores the various post-operation activities, including debriefings, incident recording, and data management. Chapter 6 then examines the case trajectories and how cases are managed when SAR resources are released from missing persons cases or if the file is transferred to another organization or different in-agency units/personnel. Cases not resolved by way of SAR response, including cold cases, and if and how SAR continues to play a role in these, are next explored. It finally examines the challenges and successes that commonly impact police SAR work as contextual considerations for the factors affecting the location of an individual.

Chapter 7 offers an outroduction to police SAR work, concluding the stories shared throughout the book and the improvements to police SAR. It presents the future directions or trends in the field of SAR, linking to existing topical issues and challenges faced in Canada and policing, more broadly, and then specifically SAR. With this, it addresses the question of "what may be next?" in the police SAR response to missing persons in Canada.

References

Atter, H. (2021). *This is what happened during the search for Burton Winters*. Retrieved from https://www.cbc.ca/news/canada/newfoundland-labrador/burton-winters-timeline-1.6172200

Bittner, E. (1990). *Aspects of police work*. Northeastern University Press.

British Columbia. (2014). *Missing persons act*. Retrieved from King's Printer for British Columbia website: https://www.bclaws.gov.bc.ca/civix/document/id/complete/statreg/14002_01

Canada's Missing. (2014). *Report a missing person/unidentified remains*. Retrieved from https://www.canadasmissing.ca/report-signale/index-eng.htm

Canada's Missing. (2022). *Background – 2022 fast fact sheet*. Retrieved from https://www.canadasmissing.ca/pubs/2022/index-eng.htm

Canadian Coast Guard Auxiliary (CCGA). (2022). *The Canadian coast guard auxiliary – about us*. Retrieved from https://ccga-gcac.ca/about-us/

Civil Air Search and Rescue Association (CASARA). (2022). *What we do*. Retrieved from https://www.casara.ca/en/casara

Cooper, D. C. (2005). *Fundamentals of search and rescue*. Jones & Bartlett Learning.

Cornell, E. H., & Hill, K. A. (2005). The problem of lost children. In C. Spencer & M. Blades (Eds.), *Children and their environments: Learning, using, and designing spaces*. Cambridge University Press.

Denver, M., Perez, J., & Aguirre, B. E. (2007). Local search and rescue teams in the United States. *Disaster Prevention and Management, 16*(4), 503–512.

Ferguson, L. (2022). "Giving the highest chance of a good outcome": Exploring the missing persons act in British Columbia and Ontario from the policing perspective. *Canadian Journal of Criminology and Criminal Justice, 64*(4), 69–87.

Ferguson, L., & Gaub, J. E. (2021). Training police search and rescue teams: Implications for missing persons work. *Criminology & Criminal Justice, 23*, 431. https://doi.org/10.1177/17488958211057380

Ferguson, L., Gaub, J. E., & Huey, L. (2021). Exploring the roles and function of police search and rescue teams in Canadian agencies. *Policing: A Journal of Policy and Practice, 15*(3), 1701–1712.

Foo. (2012). *What is the definition of "Missing People"?* Retrieved from http://www.qcmpn.com/definition-of-a-missing-person.html#:~:text=Lost%20Person%3A,not%20know%20where%20they%20are

Government of Canada. (1996). *Police procedures for ground search and rescue for lost and missing persons*. Retrieved from https://www.publicsafety.gc.ca/lbrr/archives/hv%206762.c2%20p6-eng.pdf

Government of Canada. (2013a). *Maritime matters: International convention on maritime search and rescue, 1979 (with annex)*. Retrieved from https://publications.gc.ca/site/fra/9.823802/publication.html

Government of Canada. (2013b). *Quadrennial search and rescue review*. Retrieved from https://www.publicsafety.gc.ca/cnt/rsrcs/pblctns/archive-nss-qdrnnl-rvw/archive-nss-qdrnnl-rvw-en.pdf

Government of Canada. (2018a). *About Search and Rescue (SAR)*. Retrieved from https://www.canada.ca/en/department-national-defence/services/operations/military-operations/types/search-rescue/about.html

Government of Canada. (2018b). *Canadian supplement to the solas convention*. Retrieved from https://tc.canada.ca/en/marine-transportation/marine-safety/canadian-supplement-solas-convention-tp-15211-e

Government of Canada. (2023a). *Permanent Mission of Canada to the International Civil Aviation Organization*. Retrieved from https://tc.canada.ca/en/corporate-services/policies/permanent-mission-canada-international-civil-aviation-organization

Government of Canada (2023b). *Permanent Mission of Canada to the International Maritime Organization*. Retrieved from https://tc.canada.ca/en/marine-transportation/canada-s-international-maritime-presence/permanent-mission-canada-international-maritime-organization

Government of Canada. (n.d.). *View treaty – E105240*. https://www.treaty-accord.gc.ca/text-texte.aspx?id=105240

Hashimoto, A., Heintzman, L., Koester, R., & Abaid, N. (2022). An agent-based model reveals lost person behavior based on data from wilderness search and rescue. *Springer Nature Scientific Reports, 12*(5873), 1–13.

Heth, C. D., & Cornell, E. H. (2005). A geographic information system for managing search for lost persons. In G. Allen (Ed.), *Applied spatial cognition: From research to cognitive technology*. Lawrence Erlbaum Associates.

Hill, K. A. (1998). *The psychology of lost*. Retrieved from https://www.researchgate.net/profile/Kenneth-Hill-9/publication/305044517_The_Psychology_of_Lost/links/577fd25f08ae9485a439b09f/The-Psychology-of-Lost.pdf

Huey, L. (2019). *An absence of evidence: Mapping the evidence/gaps, themes and other issues with Canadian research on missing persons*. Retrieved from https://8e5a70b5-92aa-40ae-a0bd-e885453ee64c.filesusr.com/ugd/681ae0_aa4eb14907cb4916a91216ea6216cf37.pdf

Igloliorte, J. J. (2021a). *Public inquiry respecting ground search and rescue for lost and missing persons, final report*. Retrieved from https://www.nlgsarinquiry.ca/files/11-30-2021-Final-Report-GSAR-Inquiry.pdf

Iglioliorte, J. J. (2021b). *Public inquiry respecting ground search and rescue for lost and missing persons, discussion paper*. Retrieved from https://www.nlgsarinquiry.ca/discussion-paper/

International Maritime Organization (IMO). (2019). IAMSAR Manual. Retrieved from https://www.imo.org/en/OurWork/Safety/Pages/IAMSARManual.aspx

Kiepal, L. C., Carrington, P. J., & Dawson, M. (2012). Missing persons and social exclusion. *Canadian Journal of Sociology, 37*(2), 137–168.

Koester, R. J. (2008). *Lost person behavior: A search and rescue*. Dbs Productions LLC.

National Defence. (2018). *Info brief on Canadian armed forces search and rescue (SAR) in Canada*. Retrieved from https://www.icao.int/NACC/Documents/Meetings/2018/SAR/SARMeeting-P02.pdf

Neubauer, N. A., Azad-Khaneghah, P., Miguel-Cruz, A., & Liu, L. (2018). What do we know about strategies to manage dementia-related wandering? A scoping review. *Alzheimer's & Dementia: Diagnosis, Assessment & Disease Monitoring, 10*, 615–628.

Ontario. (2018). *Missing persons act, 2018, S.O. 2018, c. 3, Sched. 7*. Retrieved from King's Printer for Ontario: https://www.ontario.ca/laws/statute/18m03

Ontario Provincial Police (OPP). (2019). *ontario provincial police orders, missing persons*. Retrieved from https://www.mmiwg-ffada.ca/wp-content/uploads/2019/06/P02P02P0401_Regina_Exh_127_Pritchard.pdf

Petonito, G., Muschert, G. W., Carr, D. C., Kinney, J. M., Robbins, E. J., & Brown, J. S. (2013). Programs to locate missing and critically wandering elders: A critical review and a call for multiphasic evaluation. *The Gerontologist, 53*(1), 17–25.

Pfeifer, J. (2006). *Missing persons in Saskatchewan: Police policy and practice, Law Foundation of Saskatchewan Chair in Police Studies*. University of Regina. Retrieved from http://publications.gov.sk.ca/documents/9/86185-Jeff%20Pfeifer%20Report%20on%20Missing%20Persons%20-%20Police%20Policy%20and%20Practice.pdf

Public Safety Canada. (2021a). *National search and rescue secretariat*. Retrieved from https://www.publicsafety.gc.ca/cnt/mrgnc-mngmnt/rspndng-mrgnc-vnts/nss/nsrs-snrs-en.aspx

Public Safety Canada. (2021b). *Heavy Urban Search and Rescue (HUSAR)*. Retrieved from https://www.publicsafety.gc.ca/cnt/mrgnc-mngmnt/rspndng-mrgnc-vnts/nss/hvyrbn-srch-rsc-en.aspx

Public Safety Canada. (2021c). *Search and rescue volunteers*. Retrieved from https://www.publicsafety.gc.ca/cnt/mrgnc-mngmnt/rspndng-mrgnc-vnts/nss/srv-brs-en.aspx

Public Safety Canada. (2023). *International search and rescue satellite system*. Retrieved from https://www.publicsafety.gc.ca/cnt/mrgnc-mngmnt/rspndng-mrgnc-vnts/nss/icsp-pics-en.aspx#section2

Royal Canadian Marine Search and Rescue (RCMSAR). (2014). *CAMSAR – Royal Canadian Marine Search and Rescue*. Retrieved from https://ccga-pacific.org/training/manuals/CAMSAR-2014-english-signed.pdf

Search and Rescue Volunteer Association of Canada (SARVAC). (2017). *The Search and Rescue Volunteer Association of Canada (SARVAC) – About*. Retrieved from https://sarvac.ca/about/

Chapter 2
The Organization of Police Search and Rescue

2.1 Basic Information on Police Search and Rescue

Temagami Backcountry, Ontario (November 2011) One early morning, 28-year-old Daniel Trask left his home in Waterloo, Ontario, went into the province's northern wilderness, and disappeared. As an experienced outdoorsman, Trask had made trips to the Temagami backcountry previously, spending days and weeks paddling and camping throughout the region (Mihell, 2012). Trask had spent sufficient time there such that the local caretaker of a youth campground recognized his car parked in the camp's lot. The caretaker, Jeff Geiler, had struck up an acquaintance with the young man and was surprised that after a few days, he had yet to receive a visit (Mihell, 2012). On Daniel Trask's final trip to the backcountry, he was last sighted buying local food (Mihell, 2012). Then he vanished for three and a half years.

Geiler was, of course, not the only one to notice Daniel's absence. His parents, Don and Maureen, noticed their son leaving on the morning of November 3rd and grew increasingly worried when he failed to contact them as usual (Mihell, 2012). When Geiler phoned them on November 13th to advise that Daniel's car was in the lot, but there had been no sign of him, they contacted the Ontario Provincial Police (OPP) to report their son missing. What followed was a week-long ground and aerial search and rescue (SAR) mission that failed to yield further clues on what had happened to Daniel (Mihell, 2012).

The Trask family was caught in a living nightmare. Not only was their son missing, but, as with much of the general public, they also had little understanding of the SAR process and what was involved in police work of this nature. As clues to Daniel's disappearance remained stubbornly out of reach, they were given a crash course on police response to missing persons and SAR work and the limitations and challenges of such efforts. On May 24, 2015, after more than three years of work and support from the OPP, various partners, and the local community, the Michigan

L. Ferguson, L. Huey, *Police Search and Rescue Response to Lost and Missing Persons*, SpringerBriefs in Criminology,
https://doi.org/10.1007/978-3-031-44077-9_2

Backcountry Search and Rescue (MibSAR) volunteer group[1] located Daniel's remains alongside a babbling brook in Obabika River Waterway Provincial Park (MibSAR, 2013). By this time, Maureen Trask had set herself the challenge of advocating to improve victims' families' knowledge of the process and their ability to access much-needed support (Trask, 2021). In this chapter and throughout this book, we take up Maureen Trask's challenge by, among other things, informing readers on how police missing persons work in Canada is organized as a part of the national SAR system.

2.2 Roles and Functions

Decades of policing research tell us a lot about the overall role of policing in society and how police do their job. A persistent narrative is that police protect, serve, and crime fight/solve. This, in part, stems from a traditional policing model that emphasizes crime control through law enforcement, with officers being tasked with preventing, rooting out, and responding to crimes on the beat (Ericson & Haggerty, 1997; Reiss, 1992). In reality, a substantial portion of officers' duties instead involves knowledge work, administrative tasks, order maintenance, peacekeeping, community services, and other activities not often associated with the fighting crime archetype (Bittner, 1990; Brodeur & Dupont, 2006; Ericson, 1982; Malm et al., 2005; Manning, 1977). Police have become the "solvers of human problems" (Bittner, 1967) and wear many hats to fulfill a range of roles and responsibilities. Much of the literature on these roles has focused on general patrol divisions. This is hardly surprising, as frontline patrol is the outward, public face of policing—the officers with whom communities have the majority of contact—and is the most visible role. This section focuses on filling the scholarship gap on police SAR roles and functions.

2.2.1 *Policing Context*

Recall from Chap. 1 that federal, provincial, and local police organizations have been delegated the authority for ground search and rescue (GSAR) operations. GSAR is the ground portion of SAR that is carried out on land or in adjacent waters,

---

[1] The team's search efforts, led by Michael Neiger, are recorded on a site setup and maintained by MibSAR: http://www.mibsar.com/Cases/Trask/Trask.html. The Trask family emphasizes that they could not have found Daniel without MibSAR and the OPP, who worked with the team lead on the search planning and execution. The Trask Family highlighted that the year-after-year support from the OPP, Ministry of Natural Resources and Forestry, youth camps in the area, Temagami townspeople, and Bear Island community was critical to gain awareness, cooperation, and assistance. Upon Don and Maureen's review and approval of our inclusion of their story in this book, Maureen reflected on these relationships, stating: "There were so many people who supported us, worked with us, in our efforts to find Daniel. Many of these amazing people remain dear friends." We acknowledge the work, efforts, and support of all involved with the Trask family to locate Daniel.

including rivers, lakes, streams, swamps, and marshes (Public Safety Canada, 2021). The primary responsibility of the police in SAR operations being on land or inland waters is reflected in their organizational roles and respective duties. However, also remember that police SAR depends on the organizational size and environmental complexity, which is true of much of the structures within policing (Langworthy, 1985; Crank & Wells, 1991; Maguire, 1997, 2003). For context on the upcoming discussion, this means that some agencies have no SAR-specific roles, some have select roles, and others have all that we describe below. Also, the typical hierarchical layers or structure present in police SAR teams align with the general hierarchy of police organizations (Maguire, 2003); however, the nature of this work means that these roles and functions are also pliant as police respond to rapidly evolving situations. Logically, the roles and number of personnel involved in a SAR operation develop and expand. Role setups in any given missing person case adjust to meet efficiency and resource demands.

2.2.2 Executive Oversight and Decision-Making

At the top of the role structure is the **Incident Commander**, also called the **Search Commander**, activated under the Incident Command System (ICS). ICS, and thus the Incident Commander role, can be deployed in a spectrum of emergency response management situations because these personnel have specialized training in responding to and coordinating responsibilities for critical emergency incidents. In missing persons work, the ICS is only enacted in emergency situations that entail higher risk or urgency levels (e.g., vulnerable missing persons at high risk of harm). However, many police services mirror this model less formally in routine practices, regardless of whether or not it is activated, so it is embedded in the system and guides police work. The ICS is not a part of every police organization's response to missing persons, so this role is only applicable to those services that initiate this framework. British Columbia (BC), for instance, uses an Emergency Management framework instead, detailed in Chap. 4.

Incident Commanders are generally not directly involved in the operation because they do not always have SAR-specific training, knowledge, and skills; instead, they "have taken the appropriate training to be an Incident Commander" (Participant 1005). They have five primary functions in SAR: command and management, operations, planning, logistics, and resource allocation (personnel and equipment). Incident Commanders hold overarching or executive responsibility for the entire operation, ensuring consistent and strong management, structure, and organization. Or, as Participant 9002 said, "They oversee the whole thing that's taking place." However, the specific functions necessary of the Incident Commander will always depend upon the management needs of each missing persons case.

The number of required Incident Commanders assigned to the incident varies over its life. If one can manage the SAR operation, no further personnel need to be introduced. However, multiple Incident Commanders can be allocated during the time frame of a SAR mission if it is a large-scale operation involving a mass of officers, non-police groups, and equipment. Note that while this is the case, at any point in time, there is only one Incident Commander in action to avoid confusion in command and control of the incident.

2.2.3 Roles Involved on the Ground

The roles involved in SAR operations (i.e., the on-the-ground team) are as Participant 12001 discussed: "Most of our SAR team is made up of three levels—Search Managers, Search Team Leads, Searchers." One of the most consistent and predominant police SAR roles is the **Search Manager** who has been certified and trained (by the province or federally) in search and rescue management[2] and thus has the expertise for the organization and conduct of an operation. The Search Manager is the officer assigned (e.g., by the Incident Commander) to fulfill the managerial function for the response, leading and directing the deployment of police SAR members, volunteers, and other resources. They represent the "boots-on-the-ground" operational managers with the authority to oversee, direct, control, and coordinate all SAR activities. Regarding the chain of command, these personnel liaise with and report to the Incident Commander.

Search Managers are also responsible for requesting resources (e.g., equipment, personnel) required for the case to the Incident Commander. They deploy and coordinate the efforts of all police and non-police groups working together before and during the operation, and until after demobilization. The Search Manager also typically determines the strategy for the response and the areas that need to be searched, and how to search them. The Search Manager will then allocate these areas to SAR personnel brought into the operation. To accomplish all the related responsibilities, Search Managers must be aware of and know when and how to enact the various local, provincial and territorial, and national policies, procedures, legal requirements, and partners.

Typically, once SAR operations are initiated, the most senior or experienced Search Manager will be assigned as the operation's lead to complete all these responsibilities, and the agency's remaining Search Managers will be integrated into the response by being deployed to conduct other SAR activities. Participant 1002 remarked, "We don't have different levels of Search Managers, but we have newer Search Managers doing searches, and then we have people who have a ton of experience doing tasks like supervising." Indeed, Search Managers can also fulfill

[2] This is external training held by, for example, the SARVAC, National Search and Rescue Secretariat (NSRS), Canadian National Search and Rescue Organization (NSRO), or OPP. As an illustration, the SARVAC SAR Manager training has a curriculum on GSAR regarding the following categories: urban searches, technology and specialized resources, search operations, SAR structure in Canada, roles and responsibilities, planning and resources, implementation, and post-mission and after-action reporting (SARVAC, 2016).

the role and function of Searchers and Search Leads. It can be the case that there are multiple trained and available Search Managers at a police agency, and when this is the situation, their expertise and/or years of experience can determine who will lead. Other contributors to this decision can be officer availability, shift schedules, case specifics (e.g., size, scale, necessary expertise), and the selection by the Incident Commander.

Searchers are all personnel involved in carrying out on-scene SAR activities. This role has been described as "personnel that are stomping around looking for people" (Participant 1005) and "ground pounders" (Participant 12001). Depending upon the case needs and resources, the Searcher role can also be split into **Search Lead** and Searchers, with the former being the person allocated the responsibility for the conduct of the Searches and reporting to the leading Search Manager and the latter reporting to the Search Lead and conducting the search activities as instructed. The Search Lead would direct, coordinate, and supervise the Searchers and subsume accountability for the actions and conduct of their team during the operation.

Searchers can be any individual brought into the response. One such role group is **SAR Volunteers**, who assist the police by donating human and equipment resources to the operation in accordance with the requests or instructions of the leading Search Manager. These personnel are often involved as Searchers. SAR Volunteers can also be individuals with specialized expertise, equipment, or local knowledge vital to the conduct of the SAR operation. For example, Participant 3001 highlighted that their service is partnered with a local volunteer crowd management unit specializing in grid searching.

2.2.4 Internal Program Maintenance

Search Coordinators are primarily responsible for the agency's internal SAR program, including developing and coordinating in-house training, practice exercises, and refresher sessions for SAR members, as well as developing and maintaining shared resources (i.e., knowledge management, software, contacts). Participant 1005 explained, "A Search Coordinator is usually somebody who has search management experience and is then responsible for training Search Managers and keeping best practices going, and collaborating with partners in SAR, and making sure we're doing best practices and their training's up to date." They fulfill the maintenance function for police SAR in that their responsibilities enable this work to be kept in operation by ensuring police know how to fulfill their roles and duties in often emergency, pressing, and overwhelming situations. By proxy, they procure the organizations' "best practices" for missing person SAR operations, storing case studies, compiling successful operational practices, and presenting and sharing these with all SAR members. Search Coordinators can also be involved in police SAR activities in managing and coordinating the response and liaising with the families and loved ones of the missing. They may be deployed as a Searcher or Search Manager as and when more human resources are needed.

2.2.5 Operational and Administrative Review and Support

Various review and support personnel also facilitate police SAR operations, centered around administrative and operational oversight and assistance. These roles can be engaged at any point in the case but are often involved at the onset to provide consistent, continued, and structured support. They do not exist solely for SAR activities. They are in place for police responses to missing persons, such as investigations, and sometimes general policing activities too.

Missing Persons Units house a group of dedicated police personnel with varying experience, including investigative, analyst and research, and SAR experience. Missing Persons Units act as an in-agency centralized spot for records, review, and operational support and oversight related to missing persons. **Missing Persons Coordinators** are also responsible for the in-agency oversight and support functions, providing administrative reviews of files and operational support in real-time and post-SAR activities. They may devise plans, identify new or different leads and SAR options, and formulate the next steps based on their review and analysis of the file and response activities, should SAR efforts be unsuccessful. Others may just administratively keep track of the incident, fulfilling more of an audit function.

The last is **Law Enforcement (LE) Analysts**. Consistent with the international literature on the roles, use, and integration of LE Analysts in policing (Boba Santos & Taylor, 2014; Belur & Johnson, 2018; O'Connor et al., 2022), these personnel are routinely underutilized in this work. When involved, LE Analysts provide insights to assist the operation, such as reviewing, summarizing, and synthesizing case information (e.g., known locations frequented, history, and behavioral patterns) and conducting explorations and analyses of data (e.g., linkage analyses of similar disappearances in the area). Another function is the maintenance of records and evidence to mitigate the burden of additional knowledge work and documentation activities associated with SAR efforts. Relatedly, they act as the main source for information exchange, reviewing and communicating information about missing persons, police contacts in an area, partners and volunteers, and suspicious activity. The following quotes are from LE Analysts discussing their roles and functions in supporting SAR work:

> Tracked and mapped cell phone records, searched for other missing/unidentified persons in the area the phone last pinged, conducted social media searches, identified family, friends, vehicles, etc. Contacted law enforcement agencies in areas between first missing location and location phone found.
>
> Assisting in obtaining emergency disclosures from social media with location information; mapping and predicting location based on cell phone data – cell sites and precision location data, and helping direct Searchers; and assisting in the investigation of tips and information (corroboration, actionable info, etc.) as well as general support work (signs, managing social media search pages, working with response team).
>
> Pinging/requesting cell phone records, organizing search tasks, finding past contacts of a person, creating missing persons posters, and creating maps of possible areas to search.

2.2.6 *Liaising with Families and Loved Ones*

A critical task for all cases is communicating regularly with the families and loved ones of the missing. Frequently, this responsibility rests with Missing Persons Units or Missing Persons Coordinators. However, the leading Search Manager and Search Coordinators may carry out this duty while the SAR action is ongoing as they have in-the-moment knowledge of the response progress. There is no clear assignment of this responsibility to one particular role, person, or unit in police agencies across Canada, but there is a strong emphasis on how vital this task is throughout all stages of a SAR response (initial, ongoing, and after).

2.3 In the Broader Police System

Policing has become increasingly specialized over the years, producing a pluralized workforce of officers with expert, dedicated skills to maximize the significant number of tasks and roles police are expected to take on (Heslop, 2011; Ericson & Haggerty, 2018). Specialized police units or specialty units developed as a part of such adjustments to establish specialization in handling and performing particular tasks and roles (Hall, 2002; Government of Canada, 2021). In Canadian policing, specialty units appeared during an era of increased reform and professionalization in the early twentieth century (Byfield, 2019; Kelling & Moore, 1988; Marquis, 2016). Throughout this time, reformers advocated for sweeping changes to make policing a respected, standardized profession, looking to bureaucracy principles (e.g., Weber's 1947/1978 bureaucratic theory of organizational management) to make policing highly efficient and predictable. Examples of specialty units are those formed to investigate particular crime types, like gang or sex crime units.

In relation to police SAR roles and functions, there exists a chain of command and relatively well-defined roles of personnel *during* missions. However, this is not the case outside these operations. Police SAR teams do not function as a dedicated specialized unit; instead, they are a group of specially trained officers assigned to other duties and units but selected or signed up to participate in this work. SAR, therefore, is a separate structure, internal program, or subunit within the larger police hierarchy. Multiple agencies across Canada *do* have what is classified as a "SAR team." But, for this, they have numerous police members scattered throughout the police organization who participate in SAR ad hoc for missing persons cases needing such services. They do not represent a specialty division because they are dispersed across the organization and not consolidated under a unit with allocated resources, training, and/or an assigned workforce (among other facets that make up specialty units).

Police SAR members' permanent assignments are diffused throughout the organization. These personnel are support services, existing mainly under the outfit of patrol and specialized investigative units that fulfill a host of other unrelated and related policing duties, including Major Crimes Units, Public Order Units (POUs), Disaster Emergency Operations and Planning Sections, Crown Management Units, Homicide Units, Emergency Management Programs, and Emergency Response Teams. This means that police are undertaking SAR assignments on top of their "regular" police duties, and this work functions as an additional elective responsibility:

> The Emergency Response Team for us, it's a part-time team, meaning that we have 12 members, of which I am, myself, in charge. We have two team leaders, and we all have our regular assignments, like mine being patrol. Then the emergency response side is something that, if an incident occurs, we would be called in to help deal with. So, we'll deal with everything from search and rescue to any major incident involving witness protection, VIP protection, court security. Then we also deal with things involving criminal aspects that are over and above what the regular uniform officer's prepared to deal with on the road. So high-risk arrests, any warrants involving violence, weapons, vicious dogs. I have a lot of motorcycle gangs, things like that we would get called in to deal with. Any barricaded situations, any immediate action response. Like active shooters, any hostage situations, any workplace threats of shootings or serious violence, we'd all be called in to deal with that too. (Participant 1100)

Another example is Participant 1001: His primary duty is as a Road Constable, responding to police calls for service and being the boots-on-the-ground police presence. His secondary duties involve being a Media Relations Specialist, a Drug Recognition Evaluator, and a member of the POU. Police SAR work in Participant 1001's agency falls under the mandate of the POU, which involves trained volunteer police officers tasked with responding to, managing, and diffusing public disorder and potentially violent situations. In this case, SAR work is a tertiary duty. While this is Participant 1001's function in the police system, this split of roles and responsibilities is not unique, nor is it unusual that SAR is a secondary, tertiary, or even further peripheral duty. Thus, while a range of specialists fulfill distinct organizational roles for this work, there is no functional differentiation in the form of a special unit in police agencies.

Specialization may be important for police SAR work. When work is recognized as worthy of specialization, an agency is signaling—to those both inside and outside—that it is an organizational and operational priority. Officers emphasize specialization in the broader police system may be a way to tend to some of the issues faced with SAR responses that impact cases being resolved efficiently: resourcing issues; invisibility in the policing system; a lack of agency, national, and federal support; inconsistent intra- and inter-agency practices; team and personnel coordination problems; splitting of duties and responsibilities; and a general absence of known, established, and offered tools and technologies in-agency. Participant 5002 detailed this:

> I don't think missing persons is recognized as an area that requires specialized expertise … the persons going into those roles would need to earn those spots by virtue of their operational skills and experience that they bring to the table. Whereas right now, I know that's not the case …. It's a job that requires a very strong investigational background, but also it requires a great deal of assertiveness and ability to work on not only the operational policing side, but also on the side of working very assertively in partnerships with all kinds of

> other agencies. And then, of course, the huge one is with families as well. So, I mean, it takes a unique skill set, and I don't think that that is recognized enough. Not even close.

There are limitations to specializing police SAR work. The most obvious is resource allocation, which is a two-pronged problem. The first prong is task segmentation and sub-specialization. Missing persons cases require a diverse set and combination of resources; one may require K9 (canine) Searchers and aerial backup, whereas another may need marine patrol assistance. The nuanced and complex nature of missing persons reports requiring SAR services means that responses are case by case. Another prong is that specialization only sometimes results in creating a dedicated unit, particularly among smaller agencies. Small- and medium-sized agencies often do not have specialized police units because of the sporadic need for specialized work. Rather, a larger contingent of certified officers would be permanently housed throughout the organization.

In sum, SAR work is typically peripheral, and police SAR personnel, regardless of their roles and responsibilities, are dispersed throughout various areas of policing. While there are distinct reporting relationships, roles, functions, and responsibilities during SAR operations, this work is not treated as a specialized assignment in the broader police system.

References

Belur, J., & Johnson, S. (2018). Is crime analysis at the heart of policing practice? A case study. *Policing and society, 28*(7), 768–786.

Bittner, E. (1967). *The police on skid-row: A study of peace keeping* (Vol. 32, p. 699). Ardent Media.

Bittner, E. (1990). *Aspects of police work*. Northeastern University Press.

Boba Santos, R., & Taylor, B. (2014). The integration of crime analysis into police patrol work: Results from a national survey of law enforcement agencies. *Policing: an international journal of police strategies & management, 37*(3), 501–520.

Brodeur, J. P., & Dupont, B. (2006). Knowledge workers or "knowledge" workers? *Policing and Society, 16*(1), 7–26.

Byfield, N. P. (2019). Race science and surveillance: Police as the new race scientists. *Social Identities, 25*(1), 91–106.

Crank, J. P., & Wells, E. L. (1991). The effects of size and urbanism on structure among Illinois police departments. *Justice Quarterly, 8*, 169–185.

Ericson, R. V. (1982). *Reproducing order: A study of police patrol work* (Vol. 5). University of Toronto Press.

Ericson, R. V., & Haggerty, K. D. (1997). *Policing the risk society*. University of Toronto Press.

Ericson, R. V., & Haggerty, K. D. (2018). Securities. In *Policing the risk society* (pp. 197–222). University of Toronto Press.

Government of Canada. (2021). *Police discretion with young offenders: Organizational factors affecting police discretion*. Retrieved January 28, 2023, from https://www.justice.gc.ca/eng/rp-pr/cj-jp/yj-jj/discre/org/special.html

Hall, D. T. (2002). *Careers in and out of organizations*. Sage.

Heslop, R. (2011). The British police service: Professionalisation or 'McDonaldization'? *International Journal of police science & Management, 13*(4), 312–321.

Kelling, G. L., & Moore, M. H. (1988). The evolving strategy of policing: Perspectives on policing. In *US Department of Justice, National Institute of Justice*. Pearson.

Langworthy, R. (1985). Research note: Wilson's theory of police behavior: A replication of the constraint theory. *Justice Quarterly, 2*, 89–98.
Maguire, E. R. (1997). Structural change in large municipal police organizations during the community policing era. *Justice Quarterly, 14*, 701–730.
Maguire, E. R. (2003). *Organizational structure in American police agencies: Context, complexity, and control*. SUNY Press.
Malm, A., Pollard, N., Brantingham, P., Tinsley, P., Plecas, D., Brantingham, P., et al. (2005). *A 30 year analysis of police service delivery and costing: "E" division*. Centre for Criminal Justice Research.
Manning, P. K. (1977). *Police work: The social organization of policing* (Vol. 439, No. 1, p. 189). MIT Press.
Marquis, G. (2016). 7. Vancouver vice: The police and the negotiation of morality, 1904–1935. In *Essays in the history of Canadian law* (pp. 242–273). University of Toronto Press.
Michigan Backcountry Search and Rescue (MibSAR). (2013). *Daniel Trask's home page*. Retrieved from http://www.mibsar.com/Cases/Trask/Trask.html
Mihell, C. (2012). Into the light. *Explorer Magazine* (pp. 64–79). Fall 2012.
O'Connor, C. D., Ng, J., Hill, D., & Frederick, T. (2022). Thinking about police data: Analysts' perceptions of data quality in Canadian policing. *The Police Journal, 95*(4), 637–656.
Public Safety Canada. (2021). *National Search and Rescue Secretariat*. Retrieved from https://www.publicsafety.gc.ca/cnt/mrgnc-mngmnt/rspndng-mrgnc-vnts/nss/nsrs-snrs-en.aspx
Reiss Jr, A. J. (1992). Police organization in the twentieth century. *Crime and Justice, 15*, 51–97.
SARVAC. (2016). *Training curriculum standards for ground search and rescue operations: Searcher, team leader, and SAR manager*. Retrieved February 1, 2023, from https://sarvac.ca/wp-content/uploads/2016/10/Z1625-16_EN.pdf
Trask, M. (2021). *Missing persons from the families perspective*. Retrieved from https://www.missingpersonsresearchhub.com/post/missing-persons-from-the-families-perspective.
Weber, M. (1947). *The theory of social and economic organization*. Oxford University Press.
Weber, M. (1978). Bureaucracy. In *Economy and society: An outline of interpretive sociology* (G. Roth, & C. Wittich, Trans. and Ed.). University of California Press.

Chapter 3
The Launch of Police Search and Rescue Response

3.1 The 24-Hour Myth

Whitehorse, Yukon (January 2022) It is every parent's worst nightmare: a momentary distraction and their child is gone. This scenario—the stuff of movies and television shows—is, unfortunately, the experience of thousands of parents each year whose children go missing. It was also the fate of one Yukon family. On an unusually warm January day in the Whistle Bend neighborhood of Whitehorse, this family was taking advantage of the weather and enjoying some time outside. During this, their four-year-old son disappeared, likely having wandered away (Elliot, 2022). They promptly called 9-1-1 at 1:05 PM, following which the Whitehorse detachment of the Royal Canadian Mounted Police (RCMP) received the report (RCMP, 2022).

Within one hour, the RCMP had mustered police Searchers, called in the local non-police SAR volunteer team, and engaged a helicopter in the response. Police traffic officers were deployed to set up check stops of vehicles exiting popular routes out of the neighborhood, while the RCMP's "M" Division Police Dog Services (PDS) was sent to track the child with dog Searchers (Elliot, 2022). At 2:23 PM, the boy was located safe and well by the Police Service Dog, Duke, and his handler, Corporal Cam Long (RCMP, 2022).

In cases involving vulnerable individuals—children, older adults, or those with serious medical conditions—it might seem an obvious reaction for most people to immediately alert the police. But many are less aware of the necessity of quickly filing a police report for all types of missing persons, not just vulnerable persons. As this story demonstrates, initiating a report can involve someone calling the police via 9-1-1 if they notice a person is gone. Reports need to be made as soon as an individual is noticed as missing; however, a widespread myth about missing persons cases, perpetuated by crime and policing entertainment (e.g., shows like Crime

L. Ferguson, L. Huey, *Police Search and Rescue Response to Lost and Missing Persons*, SpringerBriefs in Criminology,
https://doi.org/10.1007/978-3-031-44077-9_3

Scene Investigation (CSI) and The First 48), is that 24 or 48 hours, or some other arbitrary amount of time, must pass before filing a report with the police (Ferguson, 2022; Phillips, 2022):

> There's still a common misunderstanding that a person has been missing for 24 hours before they can be reported missing. That is 100% not true. That's American television, and we still have people that sit by the phone waiting for the clock to change to the 24-hour time period, and then they call in and say, "My wife went missing. It was 4 o'clock yesterday afternoon," and you're like that was 24 hours ago, and they'll say, "I thought we had to wait." That is not true at all … Literally, a person can be missing for a matter of minutes, and it could get reported missing. We need to know that sooner rather than later. (Participant 1007)

This myth did not appear out of thin air; there is speculation that some police services held this "rule" informally in the past to manage resources and because most missing people return within 24–48 hours. Nonetheless, this is not current practice because of the potential impact time can have on cases. It can be detrimental to the police response if a lot of (even a little) time passes without calling the police. Every second, minute, hour, day can count. While the clock ticks on, trails, traces, leads, and evidence can disappear, and it becomes more likely that people will forget or jumble details and information. Time delays also mean higher chances of missing people wandering or traveling further and longer exposure to the elements. This is lost time the police could have spent looking for the individual. From a policing perspective, the greater the time that elapses between a person's disappearance and police involvement, the more resources will be needed to locate the missing person. The call for police service is, therefore, a significant moment in a missing persons case that can greatly affect police response and case outcomes.

This chapter explores the initiation of police involvement in missing persons cases, starting with The Call.

3.2 The Call

If police are conducting a SAR operation, then at earlier times, a missing persons report must have been filed. At some moment, someone must have called the police to file a report because their colleague, friend, sister, father, or loved one was not where they were expected to be. Citizen calls to the police generally pass through two important functions in emergency services: a call-taker and dispatch. Emergency call-takers and dispatchers (ECDs) are located in emergency control centers and learn about missing persons via telephone and radio systems; this is where their involvement in cases ends too. Their role in missing persons cases is the same as all other crime and social-related incidents: accepting emergency calls for police service, receiving and transmitting pertinent information, liaising between citizens and police, dispatching available police personnel, and guiding the caller through the next steps (Kindermann et al., 2020; Simpson, 2021; Załuski & Makara-Studzińska, 2022). ECDs are thus one of the first points of contact for citizens reporting people as missing, representing "the vital link between needing help and receiving help"

(Simpson, 2021, p. 1). Police SAR, for the most part, cannot be launched without ECD involvement and the call for police response. Although, people can also visit police stations, flag down an officer in the community, or call the police service non-emergency line.

The difference between a call-taker and dispatch is noted by Participant 1002: "The call taker will take all of the information, send it up to the communications room and then dispatch, they will dispatch a patrol car to go out to the scene where that person is calling to initiate an investigation relating to that missing person." A call-taker speaks with the citizen who dialled 9-1-1, liaising between them and dispatch. A dispatcher is responsible for receiving and transmitting the information gathered by the call-taker. They are also tasked with guiding the appropriate type and number of resources required to respond to cases as viewed as necessary at this early stage with the limited information they have. Dispatch thus liaises between the call-taker and the police department. Dispatch can also act as the call-taker, occurring primarily in smaller centers.

When calling the police, people are asked an array of questions by call-takers to capture relevant information that can inform what police resources are required, assign priority to the report, and steer police response. Let us break down a script of a call-taker and a citizen. This came through as a missing persons call involving an elderly male—pseudonym "Mike"—with mild-but-worsening dementia; the complainant (reportee; person making the call) was his daughter—pseudonym "Jane." Jane was concerned as she had not heard from Mike in more than eight hours, which was unusual for their relationship. She was also worried because he had a history of disappearing or taking off because of memory issues stemming from dementia. The last few times Mike had gotten lost, he had taken longer to make it home but had always made it home. This time, it was different.

Although it was not the only incident of Mike going missing, it was the first time Jane had involved the police in locating him. First, the call-taker sought to establish when Mike was last in contact with Jane:

> Call-taker: When did your father go missing?
>
> Jane: 20 to 10 this morning … That was the last time I spoke to him. He was sitting in his van, and I entered the directions to the doctor's office in his GPS. I pressed enter, and it said to proceed to [location redacted], and I thought, "ok, he's good to go." Of course, that was after I gave him all the directions, and he said, "I'll never find that."

The call-taker then tried to find out a potential place last seen (PLS) or place last known (PLK) (more on these in Chap. 4) to be verified by the responding police officers:

> Call-taker: Where is his doctor's office?
>
> Jane: It's Doctor [name redacted] on [location redacted]. Right where [location redacted]. I don't know the address. The doctor he was going to today was Doctor [name redacted] … He may have thought he was going to the other doctor … his old Doctor.

Following this, attention turns to capturing contextual and incident information that may be useful for attempting to locate Mike in and by the community and police:

> Call-taker: What was he driving?

Jane: 2003 Grand Caravan, Blueish Silver.

Call-taker: Are there any distinguishing features on the van?

Jane: On the back, it says [name redacted] and has a skirt on the back … and it has been modified for a ramp in the back.

Call-taker: What was he wearing?

Jane: Green windbreaker with blue trim. Clunky black orthopaedic shoes. Possibly grey pants … yeah, I'm not entirely sure.

These pieces of information are what the public sees in missing persons appeals on social media and in the news. The call-taker also gathers some information on potential locations Mike may be for the police to begin the response:

Call-taker: How long has he lived at this residence?

Jane: Since 1981.

Call-taker: Where did he live before?

Jane: In [location redacted] for six years. 1975-1981 he lived in [location redacted]. But that doesn't live in his memory. What he remembers, though, is growing up in [location redacted]. He remembers a few things from [location redacted].

Call-taker: Did he work in [location redacted]?

Jane: He was an HR Manager at [employment redacted]. He retired 25 years ago.

Call-taker: What places does he remember in [location redacted] the most?

Jane: Costco, Food Basics … my house … and my brother's house … and his barber.

Call-taker: Where is his barber?

Jane: [Located redacted], the little strip mall where the Giant Tiger is.

Call-taker: What Costco does he use?

Jane: The one just north of [located redacted].

Call-taker: What Food Basics does he use?

Jane: [Location redacted].

Call-taker: What is your brother's address?

Jane: [Location redacted]. Belinda, his wife, is at work today, and Connor, my brother, will be here in about five minutes.

These places would be marked as points of interest for police follow-up during the response. The call-taker proceeds to capture some potential behavioral patterns:

Call-taker: If he gets lost, what does he do?

Jane: Drive until he figures he will have gone too far. It took him 40 minutes to drive home one night.

Call-taker: What will he do when he's gone too far?

Jane: Well, he doesn't have his cell phone on him, so he will go to a gas station and ask for directions.

And any other places beyond those already discussed that the police might visit and/or search:

Call-taker: Does he have any friends he would visit or contact?
Jane: No.

Call-taker: What about any hobbies?
Jane: Nothing.

Understanding his behavior helps the call-taker establish what Mike normally does when he is lost. His medical history is then interrogated to gauge health and well-being vulnerabilities:

Call-taker: Is he able to walk well?
Jane: Oh yeah, and fast.

Call-taker: What can you tell me about his medical history?
Jane: He's had three heart attacks. The last was in 1996; he had a triple bypass. He also had prostate cancer around 2000. He takes medication for cholesterol and blood pressure, and he also takes pills for his memory. If he doesn't take those, he gets foggy.

Lastly, the call-taker gives space for Jane to offer any other undisclosed details; in this case, Jane gave another address to check out:

Call-taker: Anything else you can think of?
Jane: I don't believe so. Oh, he would go to his bank. Bank of Montreal, near [location redacted].

This call log represents one questioning sequence of missing persons police service calls. That said, call-takers can ask a myriad of questions, all of which depend upon the unfolding case particulars, missing person characteristics, and potential risk or vulnerability factors being reported. For example, the types of questions for a missing persons service call involving a three-year-old toddler would be different from those of an elderly male. For the former, there would be questions about if there would be any reason to suspect the toddler may have been abducted or kidnapped, their ability to communicate, the nature of the parent or guardian's involvement, and why and how they were able to disappear, among others.

While the reportee is disclosing details, the call-taker is inputting this information into what is known as a Computer-Aided Dispatch (CAD) system, which receives calls for service and dispatches the police. ECDs utilize CAD systems to prioritize and record incident calls, identify the status and location of police in the field, and appropriately and effectively dispatch police personnel. At the same time as information is being captured in the CAD system, ECDs are loosely categorizing the case based on the details to engage in decision-making related to the dispatch of police resources. One-way calls are categorized to inform police response is the type of call. The following call-type categories are those in which our CAD data of crime- and social-related service calls involved a missing persons incident:

- MISSING PERSON
- CHECK WELFARE
- TROUBLE WITH PERSON
- SECTION 11—MENTAL HEALTH ACT

- ASSIST OTHER AGENCY
- ASSIST PUBLIC
- DOMESTIC DISPUTE/DOMESTIC BREACH
- ESCAPE CUSTODY/UNLAW AT LARGE/BAIL VIOLATION
- OVERDOSE/ATTEMPT SUICIDE
- SEXUAL ASSAULT
- SUSPICIOUS PERSON

Why do these cases have various call-type categories instead of just "missing person"? As another study on police CAD data discovered, police service calls are generally categorized by either incident or offense type(s), but sometimes not both:

> Offence-based occurrences label investigations into the contravention of enforceable law, while incident-based events are suspicious non-offence-related investigations and/or address public safety concerns … RMS are structured to prioritize the offence category over the incident category. Thus, files that intersect with a law enforcement provision will be reindexed in a naming convention within police RMS as something other than "missing person." This makes practical sense from a police perspective to trigger a series of required actions and procedures, such as transferring the file to a more felicitous or specialized policing area for further investigation, apprehension of an offender, and/or case closure … This does not mean that the person is not missing; it represents the recognition that the case has complexity, warranting particular attention from dedicated officers and resources. (Ferguson et al., 2023, p. 6)

Cases involving connections beyond just being missing (e.g., criminal incidents or ties, or the potential for which) can be classified as something other than "missing person" to involve the most appropriate police resources. This means that service calls for missing persons are treated as "missing person" until/if there is suspicion, mention, or evidence of criminality, at which time the ECDs would dispatch the call based on the criminal incident instead, like "sexual assault" or "domestic dispute" as documented above, while also noting the missing event in the log.

Another way calls are classified for police response is based on priority. That is, reportee-reported information gathered by ECDs is used to engage in a rudimentary, initial priority assessment. Such assessments occur to handle the influx of requests for police service by triaging and determining the urgency of calls based on the need for quick response versus responding to calls sequentially as they come in. There has been a growing number of calls for police service and the percentage of service calls requiring the dispatch of a police officer over the last decade or so (Malm et al., 2005; Huey et al., 2016; Koziarski et al., 2022; see also Statistics Canada, 2013). Non-urgent cases still receive a response; police focus on the most urgent first.

The general ways in which missing persons cases are priority classified are based on numbering or labelling systems, such as 1 = Most Serious (meaning imminent loss of life) to 6 or 8 = Least Serious (meaning non-emergency), or (1) Routine, (2) Low Priority, and (3) Priority. Routine or Least Serious service calls are those not requiring an immediate police response, such as minor crimes with no present suspects, incidents not involving violence or risk to the public, or incidents with no potential for escalation. Low-Priority service calls are minor incidents where the timeliness of police response is considered not to be an issue. Lastly, Priority or Most Serious service calls are urgent incidents that need an immediate police response, including incidents requiring medical attention, death investigations, incidents involving danger or risk, or crimes in progress. Given that time is of the essence for missing persons cases and the often-high risk of vulnerability and harm, the majority tend to be classified as Priority. To illustrate, we located just 866 missing person files classified as Routine or Low Priority over six years of police CAD records, representing just 1.3% of all service calls and 34.1% of missing persons service calls specifically.[1] However, cases may be regarded as Routine or Low Priority if there are no broad concerns over their whereabouts or their and the community's safety and well-being.

Following these processes, dispatch decision-making regarding what resources are needed for the case then occurs. Part of this involves evaluating if there is enough information to provide the police grounds to respond, as there can be vast discrepancies in the nature of service calls. It might be the case that more information must be gathered to determine what, if any, type of police response is appropriate. A call for police service does not always mean police response. However, if it is determined that police response is warranted, dispatch then pushes out the call for service to the local police department with jurisdiction via the CAD interface. However, sometimes calls are emergency situations that require the nearest officers available, regardless of jurisdiction assignment. Routine and Low-Priority calls are typically held until an officer responsible for the jurisdiction, or the particular case type, becomes available. Examples of CAD missing person dispatches requiring response pushed out to police departments are as follows:

> COMPLAINANT'S DAUGHTER [MISSING PERSON NAME REDACTED]—15 YRS OLD—WAS OUT WITH A FRIEND LAST NIGHT—HASN'T HEARD FROM HER SINCE—FRIEND BELIEVES SHE WENT TO [ADDRESS REDACTED] — COMPLAINANT SAID MALE FRIEND WENT TO LOOK FOR HER AT THAT APARTMENT AND WAS BUZZING 1264—OLDER MALES CAME OUT AND THREATENED TO BEAT HIM UP.

> TWO GRADE 8 STUDENTS. LAST SEEN 20 MIN AGO [MISSING PERSON #1 NAME REDACTED] (FEMALE), LONG BLONDE HAIR WITH BANGS, 5'5, STOCKY BUILD, [HOME ADDRESS REDACTED] AND [MISSING PERSON #2 NAME REDACTED] (FEMALE) SHOULDER-LENGTH BROWN HAIR WITH RED IN IT. 5'4, MEDIUM BUILD [HOME ADDRESS REDACTED]. LIKELY WALKED OFF TOGETHER.

> COMPLAINANT ARRIVED HOME TO FIND HER GIRLFRIEND [MISSING PERSON NAME REDACTED] AND DAUGHTER [MISSING CHILD NAME REDACTED] —4 YRS OLD—BOTH ARE GONE—A SUICIDE NOTE WAS LEFT BEHIND—CELL PHONE GOES STRAIGHT TO VOICEMAIL.

3.3 Initial Response

After ECDs push out the service call, police receive a message initiated by CAD systems to their vehicle mobile device terminals (MDTs) (i.e., computers within patrol cars), radios, and work cell phones. There are multiple communication

---

[1] These numbers are not generalizable or verifiable beyond our data.

options to ensure the flow of information. At this stage, a response will be initiated by engaging an Initial Responding Officer (also referred to as the Investigating Officer or IO). This officer, perhaps officers, is designated with responsibility for conducting an initial investigation. They are typically assigned by dispatch based on standing procedures or specific to the case; contributing factors to this designation decision can be, for example, the police resources available and their proximity to the incident and/or reportee.

IOs can be any police member on duty, on the beat and available to respond. These personnel are typically frontline patrol officers. Any officer can conduct the initial response to the case, as what is required at this stage is equivalent to most other reports: Collect information, interview the reportee and any witness(es), begin the documentation process, and assess the case for the next steps. Indeed, in line with the broader literature on coordinating work in policing, missing persons files begin with information developed out of patrol work (Giacomantonio, 2015; Brodeur, 2010; Ericson, 1982). "The initial investigation is key," said Participant 1004, "because, from there, that's all your data or all the information you're using to determine where you're going to look and how you're going to look for this person." The primary purpose of the IO investigation is thus to permit a decision on whether to order SAR and what the next steps are in the case. Because, at this stage, very little is known about the incident beyond what ECDs gathered and collated, additional information (e.g., evidence, leads, witness statements) must be collected to establish that there are grounds to investigate the incident, and know what, if any, type of police response is needed, who are the people involved, and what are the case specifics. Therefore, the IO fulfills the necessary function of collecting case data to aid in determining the launch of SAR.

> Anyone can call and say, "Hey I haven't seen Joe Stevens in two months and I'm concerned." So that would generate a missing persons call for service, and any police officer on the street could be dispatched to that. And then they go start the initial investigation. As a patrol officer, you go out and, for example - Joe Stevens, you know, I haven't seen him in two months, but now I'm concerned. We get the details of like why you think they're missing, what are your concerns for them, where's the last place you saw them, why is it out of the ordinary that you haven't seen for two months?...We've to take all the initial information. (Participant 25002)

The data types collected by the IO are decision, search, and planning (Government of Canada, 1996). Decision data pertain to information collected to decide whether the launch of police SAR is necessary and, if so, how urgently action should be taken. Search data involve information that can direct police personnel in terms of whom to look for and where to look. Planning data include information that can be used to determine what resources to use and how to use them for the case (Government of Canada, 1996). These three buckets of information are garnered through various methods and processes by the IO. One is a form or questionnaire used as a guideline for establishing the necessity and urgency of possible SAR action. The IO must complete this without delay to mobilize SAR action as soon as possible if the case requires it. Filling out the form/questionnaire is the first task expected of IOs. Participant 41001 stated, "When you arrive on scene, you do the search urgency right away, regardless of the situation at hand." Urgency determination derives from a set of questions on "risk" or vulnerability indicators when missing, including the missing person's profile (e.g., demographics) or weather and terrain conditions. Participant 1002 commented that specific to Ontario, such urgency criteria were established by the various parties involved in SAR: "This criterion was adopted from the training from the OPP, and from other search groups like Ontario Search and Rescue Volunteer Association (OSARVA) and Canadian Association of Search and Rescue (CASAR)." Participant 1002 then read the 11 questions verbatim off their agency's form:

> 1) Is there suspicion of foul play and/or abduction—parental or non-parental? 2) Is the person 12 years of age and under? 3) Is the physical or intellectual capacity of the person placing them at risk of themselves of injury or death? 4) Is there a medical condition that's in place that's placing them in risk of injury or death? 5) Does the person suffer from a mental disorder, or does the emotional state of the person suggest they are a danger to themselves or others? 6) Is a person elderly or unable to care for themselves due to their age or medical condition—for example like Alzheimer's? 7) Is the person under the age of 16 years and is known to be involved in prostitution, use of cocaine, crack, meth etc., or other drugs? 8) Is the person being reported to the [police service redacted] for the first time as being missing—and the circumstances are both unexplained and a significant departure from their normal behaviour? 9) Is the person being reported missing from a woman's shelter? 10) Has a criminal offence been committed? and 11) Are there any other extenuating circumstances that could lead to injury or death?

This urgency determination document has various names across police services: Risk Assessment Form, Search Evaluation Questionnaire, and Search Assessment, among others. Police organizations have created their own based on the types of cases they typically handle and the needs of their jurisdiction. These build off of the ECDs' priority assessments by asking questions specific to how to find the missing person and to "justify the resources that we use" (Participant 11001). Hence, determining the types of police resources required for the case, if police SAR action is required, and the level of urgency associated with the case for deciding on the quickness of mobilizing such resources and actions. Given that the forms or questionnaires vary by police service, so too do the evaluation outputs. Across our data, some agencies had urgency levels (e.g., Level 3, Level 2, Level 1, with Level 1 being the greatest urgency; or Level 1, Level 7, Level 9, with Level 1 being the greatest urgency), some had urgency scores (e.g., 1/10 to 10/10 score, with 10/10 being the greatest urgency), and some had urgency classification labels (e.g., Non-Urgent, Urgent, Emergency, with Emergency being the greatest urgency):

> There's three levels. So, Level 1 is an "Emergency" search … we need to find them now. Or they're at serious risk of serious bodily harm or death. The next one is "Urgent." which is Level 2. Level 2, there's some concern that we need to find this person, and they might be at heightened risk of danger, but we're not going to … like an "Emergency" search, we're basically calling in everyone that we can, and we're searching for them until we until we find them. So, the best example would be a five-year-old boy is missing—either wandered away from his house or out with his brother or whatever, we can't find the five-year-old. But we need to find that child because they're not able to care for themselves. An Urgent search, so Level 2, might be someone that is able to care for themselves, but their son made some concerning statements to friends like, "You're never going to see me again." And then the

> Level 3, also called the "Non-Emergency," are ones that are either routine missing persons like runaways from group homes. Like they runaway three times a week, so they're missing, we don't know where they are, but based on all of the evidence we have available, they're not at any risk. (Participant 3201)

Similar to the literature on the classification of incidents in policing, urgency categorization can define the work outcomes for police in terms of establishing if action is required for the case. This activity creates or eliminates work for police SAR (Giacomantonio, 2015). To that end, another form or questionnaire is then completed by the IO if the urgency assessment determines that SAR action may be necessary. This, too, has several names depending upon the agency, including Missing Persons Questionnaire, Lost Person Questionnaire, and Lost Person Report Form, and sometimes the urgency determination is a component of this form/questionnaire (i.e., they are one activity). This other form/questionnaire collects additional information on the missing person for informing SAR action. Officer 13004 said it "gives us a rundown of habits, things that they're involved in, acquaintances, relatives, etc., that may help us, sort of direct us to where we need to go." Participant 2002 provided an example of when these can be useful:

> For example, in the questionnaire, we find out that they're a smoker and they smoked Du Maurier cigarettes. And this has happened several times. You're out, you're looking for them, and all of a sudden, you find a makeshift camp ... We find that a little makeshift spot where they've sat, and there are cigarette butts, packs of smokes ... "What's the brand that they smoke?" This is the brand, Du Maurier ... This is potentially is a clue of the last known place where they were.

The IO goes through these forms or questionnaires with the reportee and other people who have firsthand knowledge of the missing person (e.g., witnesses, relatives). Police SAR can be launched following the completion of these forms/questionnaires: "We have a template that the Initial Investigating Officers go through. And then if it hits a certain score, then a Search Manager has to be either contacted or take over the search" (Participant 1003). However, knowing the case specifics based on the dispatch log, IOs can also flag the case to a supervisor for immediate review and mobilization of SAR. Participant 2001 discussed how SAR action could be mobilized in tandem while completing the information form or questionnaire versus delaying police SAR response for further information-gathering purposes:

> Every officer who responds to a missing persons call can fill out what's referred to as a Lost Person Questionnaire. It's a four-page document that they can fill out to identify a whole bunch of different background information surrounding missing persons. Now that's not to say that that document in and of itself makes a person vulnerable. When an officer goes to respond to a missing person, right off the bat they know that the person is 90 years of age, it's -15° Celsius, and they've left the house wearing nothing but a housecoat and pair of slippers ... right off the bat that person is vulnerable and things get escalated very, very quickly. As soon as they get that initial information that the person is wandering, not appropriately dressed for the weather conditions, the officer doesn't then sit down and fill out four pages of questions. The officer then contacts the Sergeant and the Duty Inspector, and the Duty Inspector would initiate a ground search for that individual. So just to say that we have clear-cut and dry documents that have to get filled out in order to make a person rendered vulnerable, that's not true. A person can get deemed vulnerable very quickly without filling

> any documents out. If there is exigency associated to the person's circumstance, then immediately, they're deemed to be vulnerable, and the search escalates.

If a report is deemed to be non-urgent, it will not be responded to immediately unless further information is received that changes the case's urgency. Moreover, if the case does not need SAR action, most agencies keep the file with frontline patrol unless the case requires transferring (e.g., to the Major Crimes Unit if it is linked to a criminal incident):

> It will stay with the uniform patrol officer that's in-house and not out on the road. They can take all the information over the telephone, and then they do the addition to CPIC because every missing person gets added to CPIC. And then, they get added to the BOLO, which is just our in-house local records management system. (Participant 2001)

Regardless of whether SAR mobilization occurs while filling out forms/questionnaires or after they are completed, the IO continues collecting information on the case to assist in the SAR efforts and decision-making regarding resources. Ergo, the subsequent steps noted in this section could be completed concurrently while SAR members spring into action, or prior.

Part of collecting information on the case involves gathering personal details of the missing person (e.g., age, sex, height, weight, physical description) and obtaining a recent picture of them. Another source of information is taking reportee and witness statements. An example of a witness statement is below:

> I received a Facebook message from [missing person name redacted] at about 8:55 PM tonight saying that he had been having problems with his ex, that she was saying that he ruined his daughter's life, was a deadbeat dad. He was saying that he did not see a way out and was going to hang himself to end it all. I wrote him back, but he has not wrote me back. I contacted his mother [mother's name redacted], and she indicated that he was somewhere in [location redacted] but has not had contact with him for over two years. He has sent me messages in the past and not replied after I wrote him back. I do not know him well enough to know if he is serious about it or not.

Aside from collecting information, the IO must also complete a thorough search of the missing person's residence, if the home is accessible, it is relevant to the case, and appropriate grounds to search it exist. This is because it is surprisingly common for people to become disoriented, lost, or missing inside their homes. In this process, officers may also locate clues as to the individual's whereabouts or vital details that can help direct the response. For example, officers have located suicide notes, noticed laptops open with message threads detailing meet-up spots with friends, and found receipts for bus and train tickets to other locations, just from conducting thorough residence searches. Participant 12001 noted why searching the home can help locate missing children:

> A lot of the time, you will deal with young children, where parents will call, they'll be hysterical because they can't find their child ... They're not aware that they're sleeping somewhere in the home. It's amazing the spots that I've found people will use – sleeping in dirty clothes piles, beds, bed sheets, closets, vehicles, the most insane places ... What typically we find that happens is people will sort of do a hasty search in their home really quick, but they're not in that right frame of mind, and they're in there rushing through their home and their property to see if they can find their kid. Or if they're living in a townhome com-

plex, they're running to neighbours, "Have you seen so and so?" and then they're making the call to us. Some, it's immediate, like, "Oh my gosh I can't find my child." But really, the child is just at home but sleeping somewhere unsuspected or hiding in the basement or something.

Another piece of information the IO collects is whether the missing person is a part of any relevant programs or registries, such as Project Lifesaver and Vulnerable Persons Registry (VPR). Project Lifesaver (2022) is an international program designed to protect and quickly locate individuals with cognitive disorders prone to going missing, such as Alzheimer's and dementia. Participant 42001 clarified, "When a person subscribes to the Project Lifesaver program, they put on a bracelet that looks almost like a watch. And if they're wearing that, then we should be able to track those people using that radio frequency machine, the equipment." The VPR (2023) provides instant access to information about a vulnerable person (e.g., medically, cognitively, mentally/emotionally, or physically vulnerable) who voluntarily registered for the program, such as detailed physical descriptions, sensitivities about their situation, and whom to call in an emergency. It is available in Ontario to "help alleviate safety concerns for those that are vulnerable in our community" (VPR, 2023).

After gathering all this initial information, the IO may reach out to a Search Manager or search-trained officer to flag the case for review and their perspective. A Search Manager or search-trained officers might instead initiate contact with the IO after hearing the case over their communications and noting the potential for SAR action.

As a Search Manager, when I hear a case that might need SAR, I reach out to the responding officer or the supervisor, saying, "Hey, I'm the Search Manager. You need me to review this." Or, I'm contacted and asked to review this … Search Managers are all over cases so that the appropriate action is taken. (Participant 8001)

Who receives this information from the IO in the police service would depend upon each organization's processes, who is on duty, and who is tasked with authoritative decision-making over frontline patrol during the incident. One role involved is the Officer in Charge, typically a supervisor like a Road Sergeant; they would receive the IO's collected information and partially or fully completed form/questionnaire. Another is a Duty Inspector, who is "in charge of the shop" (Participant 1007). This role has assigned responsibility to all officers in their jurisdiction of authority who are on duty at the time of the incident and also the provision of oversight of all police operations, during and outside of business hours. The Duty Inspector holds a range of statutory responsibilities and thus can be notified to initiate SAR action.

The IO's involvement in the case might end after collecting germane information, notifying the relevant personnel, and completing a report on what occurred. However, frontline patrol officers can be SAR personnel too, or, in services with an ICS, they could be the interim Incident Commander until one is mobilized, so there are no role gaps because they are already involved in the case. Whether this same officer will continue with the response will depend upon agency practice, their involvement in SAR in their agency, and the required resources for each case.

Otherwise, the IO will submit all information to their supervisor for review, approval, resourcing, and dissemination to the relevant SAR personnel (e.g., Search Manager). They will also document their efforts in the RMS as a response record for all subsequent police officers involved in the case to see and utilize in the case's next steps.

3.4 Other Case Trajectories

Depending upon the case, the pathway to SAR involvement might differ. Two general ways in which police SAR response is activated were highlighted above: (1) Following the reportee call, it is apparent that SAR efforts are needed, so a SAR response is immediately requested and mobilized while the IO engages in information gathering in tandem, and (2) After information gathering efforts by the IO, it becomes apparent that the case requires SAR action and then the wheels get set in motion to mobilize police SAR.

While it is beyond the scope of this book to explore in detail, in the case that SAR action is not required or mobilized, the subsequent trajectory of the case would differ depending upon the incident. It might be the scenario that the missing person case does not need SAR but requires police investigation, and, therefore, frontline patrol and other police members (e.g., Investigators) would continue to look for the individual by following leads and gathering evidence. Other trajectories are case clearance (e.g., closed, located, returned, police response unnecessary); case transfer (e.g., to another type of case classification and unit/team); and case reassignment (e.g., to another agency with jurisdiction). These are reviewed more in Chap. 6.

In sum, police SAR is launched through the following simplified process:

Citizen calls the police and makes a service request > > >

Call-taker collects pertinent information from the reportee to determine the priority of the case and dispatch police > > >

Dispatch pushes the request for a response to a police organization and patrol officer, who fulfills the role of the IO > > >

IO completes the form/questionnaire and collects information on the individual and situation > > >

SAR can be mobilized.

References

Brodeur, J. P. (2010). *The policing web*. Oxford University Press.

Elliot, J. (2022). *Yukon police dog locates missing four-year-old*. Retrieved from https://www.yukon-news.com/news/yukon-police-dog-locates-missing-four-year-old/

Ericson, R. V. (1982). *Reproducing order: A study of police patrol work*. University of Toronto Press.

Ferguson, L. (2022). *Quashing some myths about missing persons*. Missing Persons Research Hub. Retrieved from https://www.missingpersonsresearchhub.com/post/quashing-some-myths-about-missing-persons

Ferguson, L., Elliott, M., & Kim, S. (2023). Examining the connection between missing persons and victimization: An application of lifestyle exposure theory. *Crime & Delinquency, 69*(3), 656–681.

Giacomantonio, C. (2015). *Policing integration: The sociology of police coordination work.* Springer.

Government of Canada. (1996). *Police procedures for ground search and rescue for lost and missing persons.* Retrieved from https://www.publicsafety.gc.ca/lbrr/archives/hv%206762.c2%20p6-eng.pdf [May 22, 2023].

Huey, L., Cyr, K., & Ricciardelli, R. (2016). Austerity policing's imperative: Understanding the drivers of policing activity in Canada. *International Journal of Police Science & Management, 18*(2), 133–139.

Kindermann, D., Sanzenbacher, M., Nagy, E., Greinacher, A., Cranz, A., et al. (2020). Prevalence and risk factors of secondary traumatic stress in emergency call-takers and dispatchers–a cross-sectional study. *European Journal of Psychotraumatology, 11*(1), 1799478.

Koziarski, J., Ferguson, L., & Huey, L. (2022). Shedding light on the dark figure of police mental health calls for service. *Policing: A Journal of Policy and Practice, 16*(4), 696–706.

Malm, A., Pollard, N., Brantingham, P., Tinsley, P., Plecas, D., Brantingham, P., et al. (2005). *A 30 year analysis of police service delivery and costing: "E" division.* Centre for Criminal Justice Research.

Phillips, K. (2022). Don't wait 24 hours to report a missing person: Here's why. Retrieved from https://barrie.ctvnews.ca/don-t-wait-24-hours-to-report-a-missing-person-here-s-why-1.6194556

Project Lifesaver. (2022). *About project lifesaver – What is project lifesaver?* Retrieved from https://projectlifesaver.org/about-us/ [May 22, 2023].

RCMP. (2022). *Missing child located safe.* Retrieved from https://www.rcmp-grc.gc.ca/en/news/2022/missing-child-located-safe

Simpson, R. (2021). Calling the police: Dispatchers as important interpreters and manufacturers of calls for service data. *Policing: A Journal of Policy and Practice, 15*(2), 1537–1545.

Statistics Canada. (2013). *Decrease in the rate of police strength in Canada in 2022.* Retrieved from https://www150.statcan.gc.ca/n1/daily-quotidien/230327/dq230327a-eng.htm

Vulnerable Persons Registry (VPR). (2023). *Welcome to the vulnerable persons registry.* Retrieved from https://www.vulnerablepersonsregistry.ca/

Załuski, M., & Makara-Studzińska, M. (2022). Profiles of Burnout, Job Demands and Personal Resources among Emergency Call-Takers and Dispatchers. *In Healthcare, 10*(2), 281. MDPI. https://www.mdpi.com/2227-9032/10/2/281

Chapter 4
The Work of Police Search and Rescue, Part I

4.1 Scope and Extent of Police Search and Rescue Work

Whitehead, Manitoba (June 2022) At 3:10 PM on June 17, a call came into the Royal Canadian Mounted Police (RCMP) Blue Hills Detachment (RCMP, 2022). Whitehead is a rural municipality near the Assiniboine River in the flat lands of southern Manitoba. The river snakes across 660 miles of prairie, from Saskatchewan to Manitoba, taking its name from the Assiniboine people who inhabited the great plains. On this day, it is clear and warm. The gentle weather likely made it easier for the first responders and volunteers to search the river and woods nearby, looking for a missing man.

The call received by Blue Hills RCMP concerns a 41-year-old man, Jordan Ross, who was missing from his residence (RCMP, 2022). Ross had last been seen the morning of the previous day. Searchers looking for Ross located his empty vehicle on the shoulder of Highway 1 near the river (RCMP, 2022). They combed out across the area, employing search techniques to try to identify where the man might be. Searchers included the local volunteer aquatic response team, the Fire Department, area citizens, Ross' family, and the RCMP's search and rescue (SAR) team (CBC, 2022). The latter are "ground pounders" – the term for Searchers who fan out across an area looking for clues as to the location of a missing person. For the next days after the report, the ground pounders, led by the RCMP SAR team and organized to conduct a grid search, turned up nothing. Searches by helicopter and Zodiac boat also yielded no clues (McKinley, 2022). After three days of intense land searching, the decision was made to focus instead on the river (CBC, 2022).

It is two weeks later that the riddle of what happened to Ross began to be solved. Police in Brandon, Manitoba, received reports of a body in the Assiniboine River near Dinsdale Park, some seven miles away. The body is subsequently identified as belonging to the 41-year-old missing man. How Ross ended up in the river is never

L. Ferguson, L. Huey, *Police Search and Rescue Response to Lost and Missing Persons*, SpringerBriefs in Criminology,
https://doi.org/10.1007/978-3-031-44077-9_4

publicly revealed. Only a small comment in a RCMP statement: "Criminality is not suspected in the death" (RCMP, 2022).

As with the case of Jordan Ross and most other missing persons, we can only find snippets of information on the police resources employed and the response efforts and outcomes through news articles and press releases. This is because there is no publicly available data on police SAR in Canada. The only information we have is the National Centre for Missing Persons and Unidentified Remains (NCMPUR) Fast Fact Sheets of police Canadian Police Information Centre (CPIC) reports that provide "a national breakdown of missing persons reports by province, age (child or adult), sex, and probable cause" (Canada's Missing, 2021). As documented elsewhere,[1] these data are severely limited in terms of what they can actually tell us and are not an accurate representation of the types and number of reports made to the police. The Fast Fact Sheets show that around 70,000 CPIC missing persons police reports are made yearly; however, as Sparkes (2021) writes in a publication on the Missing Persons Research Hub, "In my jurisdiction, approximately half of the missing person reports we receive are resolved without adding the case to CPIC, usually because the person is quickly located, or sometimes because there are insufficient grounds to pursue an investigation." These Fast Fact Sheets may represent only half of all missing persons in Canada. Not only is there limited data on these incidents, but even less is known about cases that require and receive police SAR response. The scope and extent of police SAR work are largely unknown.

Our data offer some insight. Of the thousands of cases police respond to, only a small percentage involve SAR action. "In [police service redacted], there is approximately, give or take, 2,000 people a year that get reported missing," Participant 2001 discussed, "Now, that is not to say that we conduct 2000 searches in a year … We conduct actual boots-to-ground, missing persons SAR for about 25 to 30 people a year." Accordingly, this police agency would carry out SAR in around 1.3% to 1.5% of missing persons reports every year. Participant 4006 mentioned, "For my jurisdiction, we had SAR deployments on 69 out of 2,895 missing persons cases, so 2.4%." Across our data, SAR was estimated to occur in about 1% up to 10% of all missing persons cases annually. Given the lack of available information for comparison and generalizability of our data, we cannot conclude that this extent is accurate. What we can say is that not all or even a majority of missing persons cases require police SAR. Those that do, however, tend to be emergencies with persons vulnerable to the risk of injury, harm, or loss of life.

SAR work can be inherently dangerous, involving a range of environments and situations. One environment typically associated with SAR is the wilderness, pictured as uncultivated and challenging outdoor areas like forests, rural and remote regions, bush, and dense greenery. Incidents in urban areas, like cities and towns, need SAR too. Urban settings have a dynamic and complex nature, often containing high population densities, structural barriers, environmental hazards, complex infrastructures, and confined spaces or spaces with limited access. The scope and

[1] See, for example, Sparkes (2021), Ferguson (2021), and Ferguson et al. (2023).

extent of police SAR involvement in missing persons cases pertain to a small but risky number of emergency situations, with people at risk of harm and/or well-being concerns and tricky environments and terrains. In this chapter, we explore the aspects of police SAR work associated with finding missing people. Specifically, it focuses on what follows the launch of the police SAR response, examining the range of police SAR preplanning, planning, and operational phases.

4.2 From Initial Responding Officer to Response

Two main stages occur before the SAR operational phase begins: *preplanning* and *planning*. Preplanning applies to the activities occurring before an incident while a SAR response is in the process of being initiated, involving information review and allocating and mobilizing resources. The incident planning stage is then moved into, with the SAR mission being initiated and details developed on how the incident will be managed and conducted. After these phases, the tactical component of the incident cycle begins: the operational period.

4.2.1 Preplanning Phase

4.2.1.1 Initiating Police SAR Response

There is no standard way for police SAR response to be initiated. SAR in British Columbia (BC) is conducted mostly by volunteers activated by the RCMP "E" Division (BC Search & Rescue Association, 2021). RCMP "E" Division initiates SAR action through Emergency Management BC (EMBC). The EMBC "provides a structure for a standardized approach to developing, coordinating and implementing emergency management programs across the province" (British Columbia, 2016, p. 9). Once activated, EMBC coordinates response activities for SAR volunteer groups, such as Whistler Search and Rescue and Squamish Search and Rescue, and other public safety responses and emergencies across the province. The responsibility for SAR is remitted to these volunteers and all municipal police agencies, each responsible for these operations in a certain region of the province (BC Search & Rescue Association, 2021). Other police organizations have responsibility for both initiating *and* conducting SAR, which is the focus of this chapter.

After SAR personnel are involved, decisions are made as to the appropriate response action needed. Officers with decision-making authority, such as the Officer in Charge or Duty Inspector (as mentioned in Chap. 3) determine whether SAR should be initiated based on all of the preliminary information the Investigating Officer (IO) collected, then designate an officer as the leading Search Manager who becomes the response lead. In this process, the leading Search Manager receives the initial information gathered by the IO.

4.2.1.2 Background Information Review

The Search Manager reviewing the information gathered by the IO and checking the missing person's background information are two preplanning activities. The latter can involve reading previous police reports of going missing, if any, to begin collecting information that could be used for beginning SAR action, such as locations frequented, hobbies, or what happened in previous events. It can also include looking into any other recorded interactions with the police, like crime-related incidents. Participant 9001 noted that:

> As a Search Manager, if I get called out to a call, I typically on my way there, driving there, I check their history with the most recent incident first ... obviously if it's 15 years ago, I'm not taking too much consideration. But if we dealt with them prior, within the last two, three, four months, I'm going into appearances and looking at that kind of information. And if they have been reported missing before to see where did they end up. Obviously, those are the big go-to's first.

Additional reasons for checking police records of the missing individual include extracting information on their physical features to know whom to look for, noting any known associates, and reviewing potential vulnerability factors like recorded victimization experiences with human trafficking or domestic violence. Background information review is not isolated to this stage of the response, but it can provide information that offers a starting point for SAR action.

4.2.1.3 Resource Allocation and Mobilizing

The decision about what and how many resources are needed is another step in the preplanning stage. The selecting and mobilizing of resources can influence the subsequent response activities. Not enough can have devastating impacts, ranging from delayed SAR efforts to increased danger and vulnerability (and even death) for the missing person to public dissatisfaction and loss of trust in police. The leading Search Manager makes recommendations and requests for resources. In agencies that employ the ICS, this process includes "the Search Manager going to the Incident Commander and saying, 'I need these resources.' And then the Search Manager may have to justify to that Incident Commander why we need this many resources" (Participant 31003). Requests for resources would thus be put to Incident Commanders. In other agencies without ICSs, resource recommendations and requests come from various personnel, like the leading Search Manager or Missing Persons Unit, and approvals by the Duty Inspector, Supervisor, or Officer in Charge.

The decision to bring in additional resources rests on many factors, including considering police duties across the community, cost, resources available, and if additional resources seem justified. The allocation of resources to missing persons cases is a balancing act of ensuring the SAR response is suitably supplied without creating strains across the service and other duties—"We still need to manage all the other crime and disorder and issues that are going on within the city at the same time" (Participant 33002). Participant 6001 discussed that any major emergency incident "takes away from the policing in the other parts of the city. Obviously, if there's an emergency, we're not going to take every officer in the city to search for this missing person, but we'll take as many as we can … That does tie up our resources." Another important component of requests for additional resources is the matter of justification. Employing resources for a missing person case has to be aligned with the situation at hand: "You have to be able to justify what you requested and when. If there's no water in the search area, I can't just say we're going to use the Marine Unit when it makes no sense if they're missing downtown. There has to be some sort of justification and rationale for requesting stuff" (Participant 7007).

The process of allocating resources is iterative. Resources can be scaled up or down as the SAR response progresses and new information emerges. In the preplanning stage, SAR personnel discussed the tactic of opting to frontload resources, allocating as many resources as possible at the onset of SAR action to "greatly, greatly increase your chance of success" (Participant 1001). Frontloading resources is especially useful for emergency situations: "If it's a Level 1 Emergency, the thing that helps the most is how many people do we have available to conduct a search and frontloading those resources. But if it's not a Level 1, if it's an Urgent or Non-Urgent case, resources are more so dependent on the information that is provided" (Participant 1009).

Once approved, requests for resources and to mobilize are pushed out to the agencies, groups, or personnel that are needed to assist. Participant 1002 stated, "Because of the call queue, it could, depending upon the circumstances, because it's a lot of moving parts, it takes them anywhere from 20 minutes to over an hour to mobilize." Delays in police resources being mobilized can happen for a plethora of reasons, as can be imagined: weather affecting travel, being out on another call, traffic on the road to the location, and personnel being off-duty. It takes time to get police, tools, and equipment on-scene. It may take longer for non-police SAR groups to mobilize due to being scattered across the region or having their own protocols and policies they need to follow. Or volunteers having full-time jobs outside of SAR:

> We have [volunteer SAR group name redacted] that we can call upon to assist. And their numbers depend on availability and time of day because they all have normal day jobs. So, if it's like 3:00 AM, they can't do too much … Well, they can, they'll put a call out, but you know, you might have two or three people, or you might have 15. It all depends. (Participant 11002)

Mobilizing SAR resources is thus not always easy or immediate. Once resource decisions are made, alerts and requests are transmitted as soon as possible to swiftly move into the planning and operational phases and attenuate potential response delays.

4.3 Undertaking Police Search and Rescue Action

One crucial process in the operation is that SAR resources must be sent to an area where the individual is likely to be located (Koester, 2008). If police SAR teams are dispatched to an incorrect area, the chances of finding the missing person "approaches zero" (Koester, 2008, p. 2). The second important factor is, indeed, locating the missing person. Based on the initial case information, guesses can be made about the missing person's whereabouts to launch a SAR mission, but this remains unknown until the individual is located. Ergo, planning begins by "going with the latest and best information and using that for the starting point" (Participant 11005).

4.3.1 Planning Phase

4.3.1.1 Initial Planning Point

Police SAR operations initiate from the *Initial Planning Point* (IPP). The IPP represents the location used as the spot from which SAR activities are planned. The IPP is usually dictated by the *place last seen* (PLS) or *place last known* (PLK). The PLS, also called the point last seen, is a specific place where the missing person was last visibly spotted or identified, such as by a reportee, a witness, or even video surveillance. The PLS is police-verified information as to the person's last physically seen location/address. Conversely, the PLK, also called the point last known or last known place, is a clue of where the missing person might have gone. This evidence must generate reasonable certainty that the missing person left the clue or is somehow involved with it. Examples of evidence that could be claimed as the PLK are as follows: for a missing hiker, a shoe print discovered along the same trail the person was expected to be on; for a missing teenager, a cell phone ping that provides a location radius based on cell towers in the vicinity; for a missing hospital patient, a lone hospital gown in the bushes behind the building. If PLK clues surface during the response, it would be more recent information than the PLS and thus utilized as a newer starting point for SAR activities.

> Participant 2001: If a guy gets up in the morning and kisses his wife goodbye, and goes off to work, and at 10:00 a.m., the boss calls the wife, saying, "Where's Joe? He didn't show up for work." Wife says he went to work, boss is saying that he's not there. Lo and behold, we drive around the area, and we find his car parked at some plaza down the road from his work. Where is PLS?
>
> Ferguson: That would be with the wife?
>
> Participant 2001: Correct. Where is the LPK?
>
> Ferguson: That would be with the car then.
>
> Participant 2001: Exactly.

The PLS or PLK can change throughout a SAR response as new clues or information come to light. The IPP, though, will not change as it is from where the response initiates, regardless of whether the points change over the course of the response. Whether the PLK or PLS is used as the IPP to plan the SAR mission is case-dependent. Some cases have information on one or the other, some have both, and some have neither at the onset; however, the important point is to launch SAR activities from the most recent and best (e.g., verified) evidence. It is generally true that a SAR response cannot be launched without some notion of the PLS or PLK. Participant 6001 stressed that, otherwise, it becomes the question of "Where do you even begin to look?" because, without such information, "it would be like trying to find a needle in a haystack." Using the above example of Joe, Participant 2001 said:

> If it comes to the same scenario with the car, we would start with the point last seen. But then we realize that Joe's car's not there, and then basically, we can't conduct a SAR until we have a point last known. Because there wouldn't be any point if Joe's car's not there, and then we check videos and see Joe get in his car and drive away. There'd be no point in starting a SAR here because we know Joe's not there, right? So, then it would have to just be more an investigative side search until we find that car. And then we have a point of last known, and then we can start our SAR from there.

From the IPP, as determined by the PLS or PLK, the police decide where to begin SAR activities. One way this occurs is by setting up a *search area*.

4.3.1.2 Search Area

A *search area* is a radius or circle to be searched, with specific boundaries or a perimeter beyond which it can be assumed the missing person has likely not traveled or will likely not be located within. Key information used to arrive at the designation of a search area include the missing individual's PLS/PLK, surrounding features of the area that could have attracted them (e.g., bridges, statues, monuments), hazards and natural barriers within the vicinity (i.e., ravines, rivers, lakes, railroad tracks, blockades), physical clues left by the missing person (e.g., footprints, items of clothing), and even the expertise of SAR personnel engaged in the case (e.g., trackers). Participant 10002 described some of these for establishing the search area:

> We have what's called a 300-meter radius, which is mapped out on the map where the person is last seen – the PLS or place last seen. From there, we try to cover off as much area as we can with the hazardous areas first, obviously, in that 300-meter radius. Now we don't just focus on the 300-meter radius because as things keep going, we expand that … There are instances where obviously you find the person that's way outside of that radius … From my experience, the vast majority are found within the area that you're looking for them. But there is a significant portion that's also found outside of that area as well. Because they could get into a vehicle or jump onto a bus or … There's so many possibilities where you just can't focus. We focus on the search area that we've established. But we also have what we call our "OW," the rest of the world, which is outside of our search area, that the potential is that person could be in that area.

A tool for establishing a search area used by some police agencies is Koester's (2008) book, which offers search radii disaggregated by different groups and case specifics. Some agencies utilize this because of the different search radii percentiles it provides based on probabilities of locating the person within a range: "He's categorized the distances from which they've been located," Participant 3003 elucidated, "You have like the 100% radius, which would be the farthest person in his data that was located such as 15 kilometres away. So that's the 100%. And then he did 75%, 50%, and 25% radiuses. We base our search off a 75% radius … that's what we search under for setting up our search area. Because if we do the 100% … then that's just not a realistic search area." The search area becomes a circle with the PLS or PLK (depending upon the case) typically in the center because it is often unknown in which direction the individual may have traveled. Establishing the radius or boundaries of a search area is thus arrived at through various mediums depending upon the police agency.

It is easy to imagine how a search area can become large and difficult to manage. As such, police may engage in *containment*, restricting the area and access to it. The SAR team may set up blocks and patrols to manage and control the search area, such as road bollards, taping off the search area, or having officers and patrol cars block access to the space. These tactics ensure that people uninvolved in the operation are kept from venturing into the area and prevent the site from becoming uncontrolled. They may also position officers at the search area border to be on the lookout for the missing person traveling outside this boundary and conduct vehicle and street checks, hence, arranging a few officers along main roads, paths, or any natural travel avenues. Doing this is "essentially waiting for the missing person to run into you if they're travelling" (Participant 2004).

4.3.1.3 Operation Setup

Tasks related to mission setup lay the foundation for a well-organized, functional, and effectual operation. This involves area zoning, resource mobilizing and organizing via task assignment, area analysis, setting up the command center/post, and establishing processes for documentation and tracking SAR activities. An *action plan* will be developed with goals and objectives for the operational period—officers explain that this plan is key to aligning appropriate SAR strategies and tactics with these goals and objectives. An *overhead team* or *advisory team* is also set up, a group of SAR personnel designated to assist the leading Search Manager in directing, coordinating, and planning the response. Participant 1002 noted, "The overhead team will have a Logistics Coordinator, they'll have the leading Search Manager, and you'll have a secondary Search Manager." Who is a part of the overhead team depends on the resources deployed for the case. Other personnel who could be in this team include, for example, a Mapping Coordinator, Response Coordinator, Planning Officer, Notetaker, and operators for specialized equipment (e.g., Drone Operator). This team creates the Action Plan in cooperation. They will also initiate a *command center/post*, a centralized spot in or around the search area that is functionally the base of the operations. This center will be marked on all maps (physical or digital), and all personnel will be notified of it so they know where to report to and get response updates and information.

The search area is divided into manageable zones where teams—typically groups of two to four people—can be sent to action various SAR activities. In some police agencies, SAR officers rely on "the old acetate map" (Participant 32002) or physical maps like topographic maps, Terrain Resource Information Management (TRIM) maps, and forest company and touristry maps to segment the area into zones by way of color coding (e.g., Green Zone, Red Zone) or labeling (e.g., Zone A, Zone B, and Zone C, or Zone 1, Zone 2, and Zone 3). An emerging tool for search zoning is georeferenced incident management tools like digital mapping. Mapping programs lay out a search area and digitally manage and document SAR activities. Participant 5001 noted that this "helps you manage the search as a Search Manager because you can have your zones and teams all on the screen in front of you, and you have the times and the areas they've tracked. You can track them and manage them accordingly." Digital mapping includes a combination of Global Positioning Systems (GPS) with computerized maps and drawings of routes, tracks, waypoints, and features of the area, like cliffs, caves, and waterways. Participant 1003 rehearsed using digital mapping for navigation and searching:

> So, we have the PLS, and we start the program, and I plug in all the particulars on the missing person. I can see where we are and mark on the map, and then I can put my circle of my search radius. And then I give a GPS tracker to all my SAR team, and they go out and walk around, and then I can plug those tracks into my map, and I can see where we've searched.

With such software, the leading Search Manager and overhead team digitally set up zones and zone assignments with and within the program. SAR personnel would then join the map created for the case via a cellphone or "GPS tracker device like the Garmin eTrex 10" (Participant 1005). Some programs also allow for live tracking of SAR members to see where they have and have not looked and manage clues or evidence points. That is, digital software can also allow SAR personnel to "tag" where a clue was found on the digital map at the specific spot to manage evidence collection throughout the response. In this way, these can also be used as a SAR tool. There are benefits to leveraging digital mapping software for SAR efforts: documenting what and where has been searched with GPS data; being able to see gaps in areas searched and not; tracking how areas have been traversed; and tracking how effective SAR personnel are in their efforts. A few of these programs emphasized in our data were SARTopo, QuoVadis 7 or X (QV7 or QVX), D4H, and DisasterLAN. Their use depended upon the agency, and each had some different features. For example, QV7 was critiqued by some officers for not allowing the live tracking of the response; instead, SAR personnel had to return to the command post to upload their maps onto a laptop or computer device once their assignments were completed to view their efforts. Alternatively, SARTopo was commended for its live-tracking abilities.

A part of search zoning and task assignments is assessing each segment's *Possible Area* or *Probability of Area* (POA). The POA is a percentage representing the probability that the missing person is in each search zone. This is estimated to determine the priority of search tasks, to systematize SAR efforts and, simply, to answer the question of "where do we look next?" (Koester, 2008). It may seem quite formal based on the name; however, it is generally just a guess by police as to the individual's whereabouts. Participant 5005 explained that SAR personnel may use the "Mattson method to segment our search area." The Mattson method involves assigning a percentage to each segmented area where SAR personnel think a missing person is, ordering zones from highest to lowest based on their experience, the information collected, and how the SAR operation is unfolding. Participant 1003 detailed, "We'd say, 'I think the highest probability area is the brown segment, so I'm going to assign 30% to that, and each segment after that is going to be less percentage,' and the greatest percentage is where we would start SAR first."

Another consideration is "focusing on places that'll kill people" (Participant 18002) within the area and zones, also called a *high-probability area searching*. This entails scoping out the search area, such as with maps (e.g., physical map or mapping software), through what can be loosely described as a topography analysis and establishing awareness of high-hazard zones or natural barriers that could "be a risk factor that could cause serious harm or injury or death to the individual" (Participant 1006), like ravines, rivers, lakes, railroad tracks, and bridges. This occurs to determine places in the search area that must be prioritized because, as Participant 5003 said, "I'm going to focus on those areas that are going to kill that person first. Like a Tim Hortons isn't going to kill that person."

> Despondent persons like to go oftentimes into a green space within sight and sound of civilization. Perhaps something that's near and dear to their heart from the past, maybe a spot where they went fishing, or maybe it's in the area where they frequently liked to walk and ponder. So, we have those two options. Did they go into the city, or did they go into this green space? Well, me as a Search Manager, when we have a ground SAR, I'm going to focus on those areas that are going to kill that person. (Participant 1005)

SAR personnel role and responsibility assignments are organized depending on need and expertise. Task assignments are based on qualifications, tools, and skill sets. For example, sending trained divers into water searches or K9 Searchers and their handlers along trails and natural travel avenues or inexperienced citizen volunteers to ground pound. Participant 9001 raised that organizing resources can be challenging, especially when frontloading occurs: "We want to get as many resources activated as quickly as you can, but you still need to be able to maintain span control of them and have a job for them when they show up. So, like, we always need people, and I'll always take more people. But you still need to manage them." One tactic discussed for organizing resources, especially in large-scale searches involving several police and non-police resources, is setting up a *staging area* on location that acts as a site for screening and organizing people. Another option is assigning a police SAR member to the overhead team as the *Planning Officer* responsible for organizing and planning the response resources. Task assignments are also determined by operational periods established during the planning stage. Operational periods involve rotational shifts being set up and assigning personnel to each shift, ensuring scheduled rest periods are established to mitigate the physical and mental demands of the operation that can impair decision-making, concentration, and overall performance and potentially compromise the effectiveness of SAR efforts.

Plans and systems for documenting the SAR activities must also be established as a part of the planning stage to track the SAR activities, personnel, resources, and clues. These tasks are, as Participant 4006 mentioned, "A critical area to manage for consistency, clarity, accessibility, and making sure all documentation is gathered and stored effectively on the police file at the end of the search cycle." These can be paper documentation (e.g., *clue log*, fieldnotes), digital documentation (e.g., photographs, infrared images), and physical documentation (e.g., putting a flag at a clue). Participant 15002 detailed four categories they typically write in their Excel spreadsheet clue log: people clues, physical clues, recorded clues, and event clues. People clues were described as any persons with knowledge of the missing person (e.g., clothing, health, state of mind), like relatives or witnesses. Physical clues were detailed as tracks or signs that a person left behind while missing, like footprints or litter. Recorded clues were noted as any details the missing person left before going missing, like suicide notes left to loved ones or travel plans. Lastly, event clues were explained to be anything that signals activity in the search area from a missing person, like the individual calling out for help or setting off a distress flare.

Usually, the leading Search Manager and the overhead team will conduct a *team briefing* to relay various information before personnel are deployed. Details on the case and missing person are communicated during this, such as a description of the individual (e.g., weight, age, size, sex/gender, hair color, clothing, footwear) and personal information that could lead to clue identification (e.g., health, familiarity with the area, favorite scenic spots in the area), so SAR personnel are knowledgeable on who and what clues to look for. Documentation processes, clue considerations, weather forecasts, potential hazards in the area, and recommended strategies are also communicated in this briefing. The SAR team is notified of the communication plan, such as radio frequencies and whistle signals to use that will be recognized or how often the command post expects the team to radio in with updates on their efforts. The various SAR equipment for the case are also relayed, including what tools and technologies are being deployed and available for the mission. Sometimes, written briefing statements with maps and a picture of the missing person are handed out to the teams. Finally, space is given to personnel to ask outstanding questions or request clarity before they begin their assignments. Teams are then deployed to their zones to complete their task assignments per the directions supplied.

4.3.2 Operational Phase

4.3.2.1 Ground Pounding

The response is now in the operational period, with the teams engaging in SAR by "gut instinct or using formal SAR theory" (Koester, 2008, p. 295). Search theory is, in essence, guidelines, activities, and techniques that have been studied to effectively employ limited resources when trying to locate missing persons and minimize the time to do so (Frost & Stone, 2001). We cannot review the body of work on search theory in this book, but we will highlight some loose applications in police SAR. The POA, as discussed earlier, is one such technique. Otherwise, SAR personnel, based on their training, skill sets, and expertise, may conduct activities based on gut instinct, as well as directions from the leading Search Manager and overhead team and "best practices" established at their agency:

> If it's a big SAR, there will be four of us in the command post and running the operation. And if I'm the Search Manager, so the guy running the team, like I'll say, 'let's throw everybody's ideas in the pot here. What did you think of this? Does anybody have any other ideas? I'll take anything,' and we'll sit down and talk about it, and if we think it's good, we're gonna go with it. If we think it's OK, maybe we're gonna go with it but not right now. If we think that it's bogus, we'll go with it in three hours … But we're still going to go with it. (Participant 1004)

For deploying resources to the operation, the task assignments are actioned in order of priority, typically tackling the areas with the highest POAs first. The SAR team engages in what has been popularly termed *ground pounding* in these segments, which, as the name indicates, involves boots-to-the-ground searching and canvassing through the search area. One such activity is *tracking*. Missing persons leave clues or evidence that they were at a specific location in the past or where they may be heading, whether footprints, items that have been dropped or left behind, and signs of passage. SAR personnel engage in "searching for clues or the lack of clues, not people" (Participant 38002). Officers distinguished between some of the easier versus harder-to-notice signs of the missing person, with the former being discarded clothing and accessories, their equipment (e.g., a water bottle, tent for camping), and other clear physical signs of their presence (e.g., litter left behind, clear footprints). The more challenging signs, however, can include broken twigs and branches, grass trails, bruised vegetation, trampled bush, kicked-up gravel along the roadside or trail, and compressed or disturbed leaves. Citizens in and around the search area can also represent or generate information, so police may stop people in the vicinity to see if they can offer any clues, such as positive sightings (i.e., seeing the missing person). The absence of clues is also a clue in itself as it may signify that the person has not traversed in the search zone or area.

Ground pounding can include a *hasty search* (also termed a *cursory search* or *preliminary search*). Hasty searches involve a smaller team being deployed into a search area and quickly spreading out to look for clues or the absence of clues, signs of passage, or the missing person. Hasty searches are completed without a certain path or direction in mind, engaging in a rapid "once over lightly" search of the places in the search area that the missing person is most likely to be (Government of Canada, 1996, p. 75). The purposes of this activity are twofold: (1) to take a shortcut in the hopes of ending the SAR action quickly by looking in the most likely places first and using fewer resources in the process and (2) if it does not locate the missing individual, the information gathered will aid in planning later SAR efforts (Government of Canada, 1996). As Participant 1002 explained, "You do the quick, hasty search, and then it is like 'we got to slow things down' … then you start taking pieces of the pie by searching through zones."

In other scenarios, police SAR can engage in a *grid or line search*. This is establishing and executing a *searchline*, the most common ground search and rescue (GSAR) pattern. It is typically initiated at an area boundary, with SAR personnel positioned in a line as evenly spaced as possible. The spacing between people will depend on the size and terrain of the area to cover and other environmental considerations (e.g., weather). The entire searchline moves forward together, traversing slowly and deliberately through the space. Personnel must walk through all terrain types on the searchline path, not maneuvering away from tougher or more challenging areas like a large swamp or a patch of prickly bushes. The searchline team uses vocal cues (e.g., yelling out) to alert about clues being discovered; if a verbal signal is given, typically, the entire searchline halts and stays in place until the finding is investigated and documented to avoid disturbing or destroying evidence.

While engaged in ground pounding, the SAR team isolates and marks clues. A clue must be protected because not only it could be important for the search, but also, in the case that foul play cannot be ruled out (which is often true during a SAR operation because police do not know where the missing individual is or what has happened), clues may be important for a criminal investigation. Evidence can be handled by cordoning off an area with flagging tape, rope, or string, notifying the command post or leading Search Manager, taking photographs, and/or collecting a clue if necessary. Note-taking on the clue's whereabouts (e.g., GPS coordinates), the time appeared, and who detected it will likely occur, as per the documentation plans established in the planning phase.

Once each SAR team completes their assignment, they return to the command post and debrief the leading Search Manager and overhead team on their findings and await their next instructions. Upon their return to command, the SAR team may assess the *Probability of Detection* (POD). The POD is also a component of search theory, representing the probability that a SAR team will locate a clue or subject in a search zone or area (EMBC, 1999; Koester et al., 2004; Chiacchia & Houlahan, 2023). It is a percentage estimation of the likelihood of finding a missing person in a particular area. Just as with the POA, it is often a rudimentary guess based on how the SAR operation is progressing. Indeed, the POD is updated as the SAR operation progresses and areas become searched.

> Probability of Detection would be… For example, in our mock exercises, we mark out a delineated area, and we've hidden 100 golf balls in that area. And then we send them out on task, "Go search for golf balls." They find 80 golf balls; their probability of detection is 80%. Or say you and I are a SAR team, and we get assigned a search area. We go out, and we search that area that we've been asked to search, we come in with our QV7 data, the Search Manager has it plugged into the computer, and it downloads your tracks on the map that has the 300-meter radius and the maximum radius of your search area, and shows exactly where you were searching. Now, I can go into my map and say, "OK, I'm going to take a second team, and they're going to go into this area and search, and I want you to focus in here because the other team was in there and, as you can see on the map, hit this spot really good but they were deficient in this area," and that goes into what we call Probability of Detection. We have a defined search area, you may send a search team in, and their Probability of Detection is anywhere from 0-100% that the person is in there or is not in there. The more teams you send in, the more increase you get in your POD. (Participant 1002)

EMBC (1999) further simplified the POD with the following crude example: "Ask the Searchers, 'If there were ten people in the area you searched, how many of them do you think you would have spotted?' If the answer is 7, then the estimated POD for that sweep was 70%" (p. 33).

Altogether, ground pounding involves police traversing within and around the search area and zones, looking for clues and signs of passages connected to the missing person. Tracking activities revealing the missing person's direction of travel can also provide information that reduces or extends the search area, thus assisting in concentrating police resources and time with newly detected information on their potential PLS/PLK.

4.3.2.2 Evaluation and Reporting

While the SAR mission is ongoing, the team is continually assessing its progress. One part of this is the reassessment of the urgency and information forms/questionnaires. Participant 1006 said this is necessary because "everything in policing is dynamic. You can receive more information. Everything is always, constantly, flowing and being reassessed." Another reason is that of red herrings—unverified clues or information that do not seem plausible or are discovered to be inaccurate or misleading. Participant 4002 discussed red herrings from the public calling the police with details about the case that, unfortunately, came up fruitless: "It's when your SAR is diverted because of outliers, right? Or calls that don't necessarily relate to what you're investigating." The forms/questionnaires are updated, and the ensuing SAR activities are adjusted as details become verified or unverified. Therefore, the forms/questionnaires are not static but are stable components of the case updated as clues and information become known to the police to ensure the urgency (and thus the risk and vulnerability) is assessed with the most accurate and recent information.

Any activities, tools, and technologies engaged are adjusted, scaled up, or scaled down throughout the SAR response based on the assessment of its progress and results. The search area boundaries can also be extended beyond what has been set up, should it be determined as necessary (i.e., based on new information or unsuccessful search progress). Alternatively, the Incident Commander, leading Search Manager, and the overhead team may also recommend or choose to suspend or terminate the operation at any time for an array of reasons, like the person being found or recovered, leads indicating the person may be elsewhere, challenging terrain or weather conditions, depleted resources, or other policing matters taking priority for the resources at hand. This is discussed in Chap. 6.

4.4 Types of Cases

The specifics of the missing person case offer pivotal clues as to the types of actions, tools, and technologies required to locate the missing person. Put differently, the types of cases impact the work of police SAR and the tools and technologies deployed. This recognition spawned an area of study aimed at examining missing persons behavior. For example, Koester (2008) studied behaviors differentiated by the individual's characteristics, such as age and cognitive and emotional state. From this, he produced a volume that is utilized by police and other SAR groups. Participant 4004 explained why this book is employed in their organization: "We use that as a kind of a guideline for probabilities for locating these individuals … Because we're trying to use statistical data to say, 'statistically, this is where they're found' because you can't just start going out there and searching, you have some sort of a plan or a strategy." Even earlier work on lost person behavior was conducted by Syrotuck (2000) in the *Analysis of Lost Person Behaviour* and Hill (1998) in *Lost Person Behaviour*. Police using these theories is another illustration of the use of search theory in SAR responses.

This area of study examines how different characteristics related to the individual and incident are linked to exhibiting and being prone to specific spatial or other behaviors when missing, such as distances traveled, paths taken, and proximity to the PLS when located. Such behaviors are generally dubious, but it is argued that specific demographic groups or case details exhibit different behavioural patterns during these incidents that offer useful insights when attempting to locate them (Koester, 2008; Doke, 2012; Sava et al., 2016). For example, in their study of lost person behavior in the Australian wilderness, Dacey and colleagues (2022) found that "an experienced male hiker is more likely to attempt self-rescue and move away from formed paths, while an older female is more likely to be found closer to the last known position and on a path" (p. 33). O'Brien and colleagues (2023) in the United Kingdom highlighted that children travel further when missing than adults, explaining that "Children deemed high risk may be travelling further due to the very reason they are deemed high risk; for example, if a young person is considered to be at high risk of suicide, they may be less likely to return home or close to where they live" (O'Brien et al., 2023, p. 14).

Officers emphasized that all SAR personnel should have some knowledge about the potential or expected behavior of a missing person. Because, tautologically, the cases requiring police SAR—and the factors impacting people's behaviors when missing—guide and determine the subsequent work of the police. While this book is not aimed at presenting an exhaustive account of all lost persons behavior theories (as has been done by others), we will note some specific to the groups police SAR interact with the most. Across all our data, the types of cases requiring police SAR action the greatest amount were mental health–related or suicidal, persons with cognitive disorders (namely dementia or Alzheimer's), and children.

Missing persons with mental health concerns were the most significant category of cases requiring police SAR. Police generally classified these as "despondents."

Participant 1001 stated, "I would say a despondent person would occur at least once a day." Some of the behaviors identified by Koester (2008) for despondent persons and persons experiencing mental illnesses were hiding from or evading SAR personnel, not travelling to identifiable destinations, seeking to get out of sight, and seeking a location that is often scenic or significant in their life history (Koester, 2008).

Police described challenges in locating persons with mental illness or despondent individuals because "the person is typically perfectly physically capable of going anywhere … We have no idea where they're going" (Participant 2002). For this reason, examining previous incidents (if any) to look for locations found before and interviewing family and friends about their preferred places to visit were emphasized. Other tasks identified as valuable for cases involving despondent persons or persons with mental illness included searching high-hazard, quiet, and/or scenic areas like cliffs or railroads; using K9 Searchers; searching locations/addresses of importance; and cell phone pings. Participant 11002 noted, "If someone is despondent and looking to go kill themselves, we know that they're going to seek out a place of solace, a place where they've probably gone before, and typically, they found a calm, tranquil spot with a nice view and they can sit there and think about life and then do what they're going to do."

Next, Participant 5002 discussed that cases of persons with dementia and Alzheimer's seem to be rising, explaining that the national aging population is, in their opinion, contributing to this increase: "We have a very high volume of dementia-related missing persons … With the baby boomer population aging that seems to be going up, our frequency of missing persons searches seems to be going up with that." Koester (2008) detailed that, from a SAR perspective, there is no notable difference between different types of cognitive disorders of this nature. Some behaviors identified for persons with dementia or Alzheimer's and other related disorders included traveling until "stuck," lack of ability to turn around, oriented to the past (e.g., returning to prior home addresses), being mobile only for a short period, and not leaving many clues as to their whereabouts (Koester, 2008). Indeed, Participant 1001 explained, "With dementia persons, they don't necessarily know where they're walking or why they're walking, they're just wandering randomly." Police noted the following tactics for locating or recovering these types of missing persons: looking for barriers or high-hazard areas where they could get "stuck," following a natural path or straight line of potential travel from the PLS or PLK, looking for possible turning points where their direction might have changed, pinging any GPS tracking programs when applicable (e.g., Project Lifesaver), and visiting past addresses.

The last most significant case type police SAR responds to is missing children. Koester (2008) categorized missing children by age range because of differences in behaviors due to developmental stages: toddler (aged 1–3), preschool (aged 4–6), school age (aged 7–9), pre-teenager (aged 10–12), and adolescent/youth (aged 13–15). For example, it was documented that toddlers tend not to respond to whistles or calls from parents (and may be unable to communicate or cry out), rarely walk out alone, and are difficult to detect as they are small. And school-age children frequently become missing because of taking shortcuts from their known routes, playing with friends (e.g., exploring and adventuring), and intentionally doing so (e.g., running away, seeking attention) (Koester, 2008).

Police typically regard "children" as those 18 years old and under. They described that most missing children are located in their homes or neighborhood, as their common behavior is not going far, unless abduction is a factor. As such, one of the primary activities for missing children is a thorough search of the home, including looking in bags, vehicles, luggage, the attic and basement, under beds and furniture, in cupboards, and other small spaces in the house. Relatedly, canvassing the neighboring houses and streets was also flagged as valuable, including searching areas where children tend to play, like parks, green spaces, and waddling pools. In more rural areas, police described setting up a search area and flagging all the high-hazard areas, such as water, bushes, holes in the ground, and ditches where they could fall or get stuck. Participant 2004 discussed some of the behaviors of children who go missing and how that steers police responses:

> Let's say you have a three-year-old that goes missing, and the three-year-old lives in the neighbourhood where seven people in the street have swimming pools, and you can see them on the satellite map – those are significant concerns to us. So, the first thing we check is the house. We always first check the house. Then we check every and any outbuilding at the house, including vehicles. It's incredible the children that are found in vehicles hiding or sleeping. And then from there, you're fanning out to these high hazards like swimming pools, waterways, railroad tracks, high traffic areas.

In sum, the specifics of missing persons cases play a role in guiding police SAR activities. Individuals experiencing mental health crises may exhibit evasive behavior, while persons with dementia may become disoriented and struggle to turn around. Children, on the other hand, may exhibit unique behaviors based on their developmental stages. Various other types of cases have been observed to exhibit specific behaviors when missing, such as persons with autism, hikers, hunters, persons living with addiction, and water-related incidents (Koester, 2008). Police understanding these behaviors and utilizing tailored response tactics have the ability to aid in locating missing people. Each case is unique and influenced by various factors, including the individual's skills, experience, social group, and situational circumstances. Therefore, flexibility and adaptability during SAR operations are pivotal, which can be facilitated by police having a suite of tools and technologies available for response efforts. Chap. 5 (Part II) thus delves into the tools, technologies, and resources employed in police SAR action.

References

BC Search & Rescue Association. (2021). *BC Search & Rescue Association – Home page.* Retrieved from https://bcsara.com/

British Columbia. (2016). *British Columbia emergency management system.* Retrieved from https://www2.gov.bc.ca/assets/gov/public-safety-and-emergency-services/emergency-preparedness-response-recovery/embc/bcems/bcems_guide.pdf [June 1, 2023].

Canada's Missing. (2021). *Background – 2021 fast fact sheet*. Retrieved from https://www.canadasmissing.ca/pubs/2021/index-eng.htm

CBC. (2022). Family, volunteers, police continue search for Brandon man last seen Friday morning. Retrieved from https://www.cbc.ca/news/canada/manitoba/missing-man-jordan-ross-search-brandon-1.6495200

Chiacchia, K. B., & Houlahan, H. E. (2023). Deriving objective probability of detection for missing-person search: Validating use of effective sweep width and associated mathematical models. *Journal of Search & Rescue, 6*(1), 1–36.

Doke, J. (2012). *Analysis of search incidents and lost person behavior in Yosemite National Park*. Retrieved from https://kuscholarworks.ku.edu/bitstream/handle/1808/10846/. Doke_ku_0099M_12509_DATA_1.pdf?sequence=1

Emergency Management BC (EMBC). (1999). *Ground search & rescue – SAR100 participant manual*. Retrieved from http://www.mibsar.com/Families/docs/BCSAR.pdf

Ferguson, L. (2021). *We need usable national data on missing persons now*. Retrieved from https://www.missingpersonsresearchhub.com/post/we-need-usable-national-data-on-missing-persons-now

Ferguson, L., Elliott, M., & Kim, S. (2023). Examining the connection between missing persons and victimization: An application of lifestyle exposure theory. *Crime & Delinquency, 69*(3), 656–681.

Frost, J. R., & Stone, L. D. (2001). *Review of search theory: Advances and applications to search and rescue decision support*. Retrieved from https://apps.dtic.mil/sti/pdfs/ADA397065.pdf

Government of Canada. (1996). *Police procedures for ground search and rescue for lost and missing persons*. Retrieved from https://www.publicsafety.gc.ca/lbrr/archives/hv%206762.c2%20p6-eng.pdf [May 22, 2023]

Hill, K. A. (1998). *The psychology of lost*. Retrieved from https://www.researchgate.net/profile/Kenneth-Hill-9/publication/305044517_The_Psychology_of_Lost/links/577fd25f08ae9485a439b09f/The-Psychology-of-Lost.pdf

Koester, R. J. (2008). *Lost person behavior: A search and rescue*. Dbs Productions LLC.

Koester, R. J., Cooper, D. C., Frost, J. R., & Robe, R. Q. (2004). *Sweep width estimation for ground search and rescue*. Retrieved from https://apps.dtic.mil/sti/citations/ADA511593

McKinley, K. (2022). Search continues for missing Brandon-area man. *Brandon Sun*. Retrieved from: https://www.brandonsun.com/local/2022/06/19/large-scale-search-underway-for-missing-brandon-area-man

O'Brien, F., Giles, S., & Waring, S. (2023). Relationships between demographic and behavioural factors and spatial behaviour in missing persons' cases. *Criminology & Criminal Justice, 23*(3), 409–430.

Royal Canadian Mounted Police (RCMP). (2022). *Update-Blue Hills RCMP searching for missing 41-year-old male*. Retrieved from https://www.rcmp-grc.gc.ca/en/news/2022/blue-hills-rcmp-searching-missing-41-year-old-male

Sava, E., Twardy, C., Koester, R., & Sonwalkar, M. (2016). Evaluating lost person behavior models. *Transactions in GIS, 20*(1), 38–53.

Sparkes, J. (2021). *Check your sources – What the public needs to know about missing persons data*. Retrieved from https://www.missingpersonsresearchhub.com/post/check-your-sources-what-the-public-needs-to-know-about-missing-persons-data

Syrotuck, W. G. (2000). *Analysis of lost person behavior: An aid to search planning*. Mechanicsburg, PA; Barkleigh Productions.

Chapter 5
The Work of Police Search and Rescue, Part II

5.1 Technological Advancements and Search and Rescue

St. Denis, Saskatchewan (May 2013) A few miles east of the small town of St. Denis, police and emergency crews received a 9-1-1 call of a vehicle accident in the wee hours of May 9 (CTV News, 2014). However, when first responders arrived, the rolled vehicle was empty, and there were no signs of the driver. Clearly injured, yet he had somehow disappeared.

Being a farming community, the area outside St. Denis comprises fields and the occasional rolling hill. Trying to locate the injured man at night would be a challenge. After initiating a ground search that turned up no clues, the police called in an air ambulance equipped with searchlights and night vision equipment (Weidlich, 2013). However, about an hour into the operation, with no leads on where the accident victim might be, and temperatures near freezing, police decided to try their aerial drone. The drone, equipped with an infrared camera, would be able to measure variations in temperatures on the ground, thus hopefully allowing police to find the man by his body temperature, ideally before it dropped further due to the cold (Weidlich, 2013). But then the man called. He told the police he was lost, shoeless, and dressed only in pants and a t-shirt. Using the man's last known cell phone signal as an indication of where to look, they again sent up the helicopter without success. With time of the essence, they ultimately decided to launch the drone, which picked up a small heat signature some two kilometers from the crash site (Logan, 2016). The man was found unresponsive under a tree (Weidlich, 2013). According to the Guinness World Book of Records (2023), this was the first recorded use of a search and rescue (SAR) drone to save someone's life.

One prime focus in the scholarship on SAR relates to the various tools and technologies employed for locating missing persons, like the helicopter and drone used to find the injured man in St. Denis (see Denver et al., 2007; Ferguson et al., 2021;

L. Ferguson, L. Huey, *Police Search and Rescue Response to Lost and Missing Persons*, SpringerBriefs in Criminology,
https://doi.org/10.1007/978-3-031-44077-9_5

Ferworn et al., 2006; Półka et al., 2017; Ribeiro et al., 2008; Visser & Campbell, 2014). This focus makes sense as SAR tools and technologies are increasing and expanding; The field is in a constant state of evolution. For instance, drones and robots for SAR are currently hot topics—a quick search of Google Scholar for "search and rescue 2023 technologies" pulls up countless articles on their use and application (e.g., Cai et al., 2022; Han et al., 2022; Lindqvist et al., 2022).

SAR tools and technologies can be alluring or even exciting. They appeal to many because of the promise to increase efficient and effective police work and attenuate human fallibility. In the broader policing literature, this has been considered the "scientification of police work" or the use of scientific knowledge and technology being incorporated into the routines of policing (Ericson & Shearing, 1986). Increasing and expanding technologies in policing may also relate to *McDonaldization*, the process of society adopting the characteristics associated with the fast-food industry (Ritzer, 1993). In 1993, Ritzer, in applying Max Weber's theories of modern bureaucracy and rationality to contemporary society (1903, 1921, 1925), outlined four dimensions of McDonaldization: *efficiency* (proficient and productive completion of tasks); *calculability* (ability to produce quantifiable results); *predictability* (ensuring that processes and outcomes remain the same over time); and *control* (replacing autonomous and fallible humans with technology). We see these dimensions being of concern to and implemented in policing, with agencies optimizing the use of technology in their work, including crime mapping, biometrics, fingerprints, DNA research, facial recognition, social media policing, CCTV, and more (Custers, 2012; Caplan, 2014; Stuart, 2013; Ferguson & Soave, 2021). The point is that the advent and expansion of tools and technologies for SAR may signal the drive or desire for efficient, calculable, predictable, and controllable work to improve police responses to missing persons and case outcomes.

On the other hand, police have the ability to "solve" missing persons reports from their desks: a quick skim of missing people's public Instagram posts to see recent activity, privately messaging missing people on Facebook to set up a meeting to check in on their safety and whereabouts, and pinging cell phones to garner an individual's locational information. More than ever before, police and non-police SAR groups have a significant number of tools in their toolbox for locating missing people in all types of situations. Yet, technology can also contribute to missing persons incidents as it has become intrinsic to our daily habits and personal lives (Fatih & Bekir, 2015). Most of us are supremely connected to our social network through cell phones and social media, such that any absence from these can lead to a missing persons report. Someone's cell phone might have no battery and thus be unreachable, or someone might take a break from posting to their social media, and it may seem as though they have disappeared (i.e., "going digitally missing"):

> Now consider the advent of technology which generally allows persons to be in contact with each other at all times and from most locations. In my view, this phenomenon has negatively impacted self-sufficiency to a significant degree, inducing an unhealthy level of anxiety when persons are not responsive to phone or social media for even a short period of time. Due to the expectation of instant contact, more people are not making contingency plans, alternate points of contact, meeting arrangements, and so on, which often results in

> almost immediate reports to police simply due to a failure of technology. Most of the countless missing person reports received due to dead cell phone batteries could be easily avoided with just the slightest bit of planning. (Sparkes, 2021)

Collectively, technological advancements in the fields of SAR and policing at large have provided police with new perspectives, considerations, and opportunities to utilize a wide range of innovations for locating and recovering missing persons. These have the ability to increase the efficiency and effectiveness of police SAR work. However, such advancements can also impact missing persons incidents. In this chapter, we expand upon the work of police SAR as discussed in Chap. 4, by exploring the tools and technologies leveraged for these operations. We also highlight some other activities occurring as SAR operations progress.

5.2 Police Search and Rescue Tools and Technologies

To repeat the overarching comment about the book's findings, all described below will not be in every police service across Canada. The various SAR tactics will always depend upon the needs and resources of the police agency, the types of cases responded to, and the jurisdiction characteristics in which they serve. As illustrated by Participant 1006, "Each search is so specific to what our needs would be and how we use resources … If you get a person on horseback, or a diver, or an ATVer, or dementia person, those are all just very different kinds of searches, so that changes how we are going to approach it." But all tools and technologies are available to every police service due to the multiple police and non-police groups that can assist and be employed in this work. As Public Safety Canada (2013) writes, "This, in effect, has been described as 'seamless' SAR, wherein all issues are subordinate to the primacy of saving a life, and mutual aid—across organizations—stands as a fundamental principle of the system." We thus present a broad view of all tools and technologies that can be involved in police SAR work across Canada.

5.2.1 Remote-Piloted Aircraft Systems or Drones

Remote-Piloted Aircraft Systems (RPAS), also called Unmanned Aerial Vehicles (UAVs) or drones, are utilized in police SAR more and more. Drones are tools of varying sizes and specifications, but, broadly, they function by being controlled remotely by a trained operator (Kardasz et al., 2016; Pensieri et al., 2020). The most commonly used category of drones in police SAR is multicopter aerial drones like the DJI M30T, although there are fixed-wing and aircraft RPAS that look more like standard airplanes (Pensieri et al., 2020). Aerial drones are a newer tool used in police SAR to cover spaces fairly quickly and reach "large areas of green space and forest" (Participant 2001), ideally in areas with a visible aerial view and not obstructed with foliage, or where the terrain is rougher and more difficult to access:

> If we were to look at the alternative to using officers to do that grid search in a given area, it would take us hours and hours with multiple officers to do the exact same thing ... Drones are very effective and efficient in searching for people and covering off large areas of open land in order to rule them out. (Participant 2006)

Participant 1002 described the features of drones for SAR as "flares and a camera on it and an infrared system," giving an example to illustrate their use: "I had a case a couple of months ago where an individual went missing. It was daytime, and they were trying to hide. But we had the UAV up in the air, and the heat signature came back, and they found him." Another key feature is real-time snapshots taken via drone high-definition cameras:

> What they do is they take these snapshots, and then somebody goes through the snapshots and looks in each picture and sees if anything sticks out ... a red sweater or something flashy ... it gives us immediately a GPS grid for that, and they know that's exactly where that is so we can send somebody in to look and see what that red thing is. (Participant 1004)

Drones can also document a missing person's location by capturing images of the scene and surrounding area for police records, evidence collection, further analysis, and future training.

Drones can have limitations, though. Participant 1003 commented, "If we have heavy foliage, the cameras aren't going to see through it. It also has a thermal camera on it, but if it's so thick foliage, the thermal won't go through it." Their features may not be appropriate for the operation's area because "it measures whatever's on the surface" (Participant 14001). Other limitations are the cost and expertise required to operate them. Drones require particular skills and training, meaning only certain officers are knowledgeable and certified to operate them. Drone usage legislation and certification are expanding to include rules on who can fly them, when, and over what areas, as well as the need for testing to become a certified drone pilot. So, many police agencies do not have drones, and if a case requires their use, other police organizations and drone/SAR personnel would be pulled in to assist. Police SAR can engage non-police partners or groups with this resource, like organizations in the tech industry or local colleges with programs for drone flying. Ultimately, drones are few in the policing system as only some organizations have them and the police operators with the necessary expertise.

5.2.2 Helicopters and Fixed-Wing Aircrafts

Helicopters, such as Airbus H145 twin engines or Air-5 s or Eurocopters, are utilized by police in SAR work for similar purposes as drones. Police helicopters can have camera-and-mapping systems with thermal imaging equipment that picks up heat signatures, some of which are integrated with "augmented reality mapping that overlays navigation details onto the images" (Participant 1008). Helicopters can be engaged as air support to conduct aerial grid searches in the hunt for prominent clues in areas that are often more difficult to examine and/or large and can cover the territory quickly. Participant 12001 remarked, "If we have covered 300+ acres of land search, it's helicopters or drones we use." In the case that there is no place last known (PLK) or place last seen (PLS), helicopters and fixed-wing aircraft can be employed to look for clues of the missing person's whereabouts to be used as a starting point. Participant 4006 gave the following example: "Helicopters and fixed-wing can be very useful for search operations which don't have a starting point if a vehicle associated to the missing person is unaccounted for … If there is an unaccounted-for-vehicle, we can search large areas by air without a specific starting point, as they are much easier to spot." Also, helicopters can transport SAR personnel to a search area/zone and SAR equipment, which is especially valuable in remote SAR assignments. Lastly, they can be useful for evacuating or transporting missing persons once located, especially in challenging conditions or terrains like cliffs or gullies, such as for treatment and care. Officers noted some differences between helicopters and drones. Helicopters tend to have more capacity to fly and cover various altitudes for longer periods, broadening the SAR operation field of view and time spent looking for people. In contrast, drones can have maximum heights and flight times that may limit their utility in a mission. Analogous to drones, the utility of helicopters in these operations can also be impacted by foliage coverage. Participant 1009 spoke about a missing child case in which a helicopter was engaged but did not locate them:

> I put a lot of reliability on the inference system that was in the helicopter, and sometimes you don't have success with that because it would have flown over this area where this kid was found. But … not being an expert on the capabilities of it, I didn't know at the time that the tree canopy could, in fact, have an adverse effect on the SAR operation. I had the helicopter go through that area several times, just never found the kid.

5.2.3 *Infrared Imaging*

Infrared imaging is not restricted to helicopters and drones in police SAR work. Police can also utilize Forward-Looking Infrared (FLIR), a form of thermal sensing that captures infrared radiation through images showing heat differences (Wang, 2003; Silvagni et al., 2017). Participant 1006 explained, "It's all heat signatures that it captures. We can use that to search, and the drones have the capabilities too, the helicopters have them specifically, but they can use that to search, like a field, and they see the heat signatures." There are also handheld FLIR units used, which are "just like a television screen on a handheld thing … They can look in a bush line, and they can see heat signatures in the bush. So, like if there's a squirrel, they'll see the squirrel, but they also see somebody lying in the bushes if it's dark" (Participant 1003). Together, infrared tools like those in drones and helicopters, FLIR, and handheld devices are employed in SAR activities occurring at night and/or in challenging conditions, such as heavily wooded areas with a deep cover of underbrush and tree canopies. However, these are "always incredibly expensive" (Participant 20001), which lessens their use in operations.

5.2.4 Other Vehicles and Foot Patrol

Another tool for police SAR is that of Argo all-terrain vehicles. Argo all-terrain vehicles are heavy duty, and police deploy these for SAR action that requires travel over land or in water.

> The Argo that we have is an eight-wheeled vehicle that works like a skid steer. We can add tracks to it in the wintertime. It's got winches on the front. And it's got a big rack with a basket on it, and there's not much it won't get into. It floats, you can even stick a little more on the back if you need to. (Participant 23001)

This was described as especially useful in water, such as "in a river because a river is so shallow, and it can move along the river with a small motor. And then once it hits the dry spots, it just climbs up on the dry spots" (Participant 1004). One officer said that their agency often mobilizes these vehicles in SAR incidents during spring and fall when unable to use boats or snowmobiles to best navigate the terrain due to slush, mud, and melting or powdery snow. Hence, the use of this tool is seemingly dependent on the environment, weather, and terrain.

Police can also have all-terrain vehicles (ATVs), typically engaged in ground search and rescue (GSAR) operations for combing through fields, thickly wooded areas, and high marsh grass. In fact, some discussed having a police ATV Unit to increase and diversify SAR and other response capabilities, involving officers specially trained in using and operating ATVs and conducting SAR operations with ATVs. Some agencies also have snowmobiles for remote and winter responses, which are useful for reaching inaccessible locations and navigating terrain blanketed with snow and ice. In addition, police organizations have bike-trained police personnel or a Bike Unit as a community policing tool, which can be leveraged in SAR operations to traverse quicker through densely packed urban environments and accessible paths, roads, trails, and other suitable terrain than by foot. Participant 1003 detailed, "If we have bike paths that we need to search in a quick amount of time if they're available, we can call them with their bikes. And I know it sounds ridiculous because everyone knows how to ride a bike essentially, but obviously, as police, you have to be trained in of course to ride the police bike. You can't just bring out the bikes and send a patrol officer because if they get hurt, then there's liability." Officers highlighted that the benefits of deploying bikes in SAR are maneuverability, speed, efficiency, close interaction with the community, approachability of officers, versatility in switching between on-road and off-road environments, and not being costly. To illustrate, Participant 7006 remarked, "Sometimes our Bike Unit people are the first to get on scene. They move through traffic much quicker than patrol cars, and so they honestly tend to reach the search area the quickest. We engage our Bike Unit because it tends to get its resources on scene the quickest." Finally, for vehicles, in water SAR efforts, police boat vehicles, like Boston Whaler or Hike patrol vessels or the Zodiac rescue boat, can be engaged, some of which were described as being equipped with FLIR thermal imaging to permit officers to "see the waters at night and in challenging water conditions" (Participant 6002).

Police Community Foot Patrol officers can be engaged in supporting SAR efforts as additional human resources to conduct the response, particularly in urban or populated areas. Officers explained that foot patrols bring value to the operation as they are generally acutely familiar with the local environment, streets, communities, and neighborhoods. This familiarity assists them in navigating through the search area on foot quickly and efficiently.

5.2.5 Tracking and Air-Scent Search Dogs

Also brought into SAR work are the police dogs and their handlers that direct, train, and work with them, typically operating under Police Dog Services or a K9 Unit. Police discussed two types of trained dogs involved in SAR: *tracking and trailing dogs* and *air-scent dogs*. For the former, police "specially trained dogs that can track down people" (Participant 14001), regularly called *K9 Searchers*, are utilized to track or follow a trail of human scent. Police K9 Searchers are engaged in SAR because "dogs are very efficient at covering area whereas humans are not built to really cover ground as quickly as a dog can because they rely on their scent tracking capabilities" (Participant 24001). When employed in a SAR operation, police tracking dogs are not searching for missing persons but, instead, following them. Tracking dogs are generally put to work in SAR when there is last-seen information or leads that can offer a scent to follow. But, if there has been a lot of other foot traffic in the search area before the dog arrives, the police handler will likely decline to be engaged because the scents of different people can inhibit the dog's effectiveness in tracking the missing person.

Specially trained police air-scent dogs do not need the PLS or PLK as a starting point; they can pick up human scent anywhere in the area and follow smells carried in air currents to find their origins (Layton & Gleim, 2023). One type of air-scent dog employed in SAR is the cadaver dog, generally used in incidents of suspected or confirmed missing deceased individuals or when human remains need to be recovered. Participant 14001 highlighted that cadaver dogs "distinguish specifically for the human scent, and they can find the remains of persons gone in the woods, or if it's a homicide, they can find where they were buried depending on circumstances." Particularly, cadaver dogs are trained to sniff for the scent of human remains and detect the smell of human decomposition gasses and skin rafts (Layton & Gleim, 2023). Cadaver dogs can locate "even a single droplet of blood or a tooth" (Participant 28001).

5.2.6 Horses

Horses are also used in SAR activities, with some police organizations having dedicated Mounted Teams. In some situations, horses are employed to transport SAR personnel around the search area and maintain its boundaries. Police track and look for clues from the horse's saddle and dismount if a clue is discovered to explore it further. Horses can navigate through terrains quicker and at a higher visual level than humans, giving a different and often more perspective on the area. Participant 33002 explained, "Without having a drone in the sky, if you're going through a cornfield and you need that higher perspective, horses are there. They can cover a large amount of ground really fast." In other cases, horses can be used to locate missing persons. For this, SAR personnel look out for horses' reactions and harness their vision, scent, and hearing senses just as occurs for K9 Searchers. Officers are trained to "look where the horse looks" as:

> The horses are very in tune to people. We had a search up in a forested area one time, where the horse and the officer were walking through a wooded area, and the horse's ears twitched to one side, and the rider looked over, and it was only the twitch of the ear, that the horse made a movement, that he looked over and found the missing person about 25 feet away. That was not really visible at first, but because the horse sensed that a person was there. It was not trained to indicate when they find somebody. It's just a matter of his ears twitched because he might've heard something or saw something. (Participant 13001)

Another benefit to deploying horses in SAR action is that "everyone wants to talk to the horse people" (Participant 3005), meaning they can generate an opportunity to gain information:

> When the horse units go in, everyone doesn't see them as police. Everyone wants to talk to the horse riders, and they gain tons of information. Having them just walk through our neighbourhood and speak with neighbours and stuff, they're able to gain a lot of information that you wouldn't think that they would. (Participant 8001)

5.2.7 Diving and Underwater

Some police organizations have diver and underwater teams or units. The names of these teams or units varied across our data: Underwater Search Recovery Unit; Marine Unit; Diver Operations Team; Underwater Search & Marine Unit; and Marine, Dive, and Trails, among others. Regardless, their responsibility in SAR work is providing specialized location and recovery response to missing persons in water, as well as evidence related to the case (e.g., vehicles, clothing). As Participant 1009 detailed, "One of the other pillars that we use for search is marine. We have the capabilities of doing marine searches. They have underwater cameras, they have all kinds of different things that they use to do a marine search." This quote highlights that one tool used by SAR personnel in water is an underwater camera. Another is a Remote-Operated Vehicle (ROV). This controllable, tethered underwater robot can be operated by land or on board a vessel to survey water areas and retrieve objects in the water. Side-scan sonar is also employed regularly in water-related police SAR. This tool surveys and maps water floors and has the resolution ability to detect bodies and any relevant evidence in water. Participant 4006 explained, "By far the most valuable tool for underwater searches is side-scan sonar. Side-scan sonar used in combination with an ROV is responsible for almost all of our underwater recovery successes." How this works is that it uses a sound pulse directed at right angles to the path of a boat to detect and map anomalies on the water floor (Fish & Carr, 1990; Schultz et al., 2013). The system includes a projector emitting signals and a hydrophone receiving signals, housed in a towfish, a tow cable, and an electric recording device like a laptop or waterproof control unit (Fish & Carr, 1990; Schultz et al., 2013). The signal returns are then processed into images resembling aerial pictures, and these visuals are observed in real-time by police on the recording device aboard the towing vessel. Put simply, it is a type of underwater imaging system that uses sound waves to create detailed images of the water floor or underwater objects.

The location of missing persons in water is a challenging area of police SAR work and it frequently involves a deceased individual or missing persons' remains:

> When we learn that somebody has gone into the water, unfortunately, it usually becomes a recovery as opposed to a rescue. We divide it into "search and rescue" and "search and recovery." If somebody has gone into the water, it's usually a recovery, and our marine has the capability to do a recovery above all else. In fact, it's the only option if somebody has gone into the water. (Participant 2001)

As such, personnel in these teams or units are typically certified divers who have completed qualification and refresher training rounds to meet legislated or policy competency requirements. Specific to missing persons, some officers described completing tests and training related to basic diving knowledge, water safety, watermanship, forensic recovery, working with human remains, stamina, claustrophobia, and commercial diving skills assessments. Additionally, the Argo tool, if the police agency has it, is also often located with and operated by Marine Unit officers as it is an amphibious vehicle, as well as any police boat.

5.2.8 *Tracking Technologies*

The omnipresence of cellphones, health trackers, smartwatches, and other wearable and carried devices presents opportunities to help locate missing persons with tracking technologies. In police SAR, there are various ways to track people, including Global Positioning Systems (GPS), Global System for Mobile Communications (GSM), Global Navigation Satellite System (GNSS), Bluetooth, Ultra-wideband, Wi-Fi, and radio frequency (RF) (see e.g., Wojtusiak & Nia, 2021). The function, purpose, and technology offered by these vary, and their utility in missing persons cases is contingent upon the individual or their stuff (e.g., their car) having such mechanisms. For example, Participant 4006 added, "Whether or not the vehicle will have GPS tracking capability will depend on the age of the vehicle. Unfortunately, many of our missing persons drive older vehicles, for which this is not an option. Similarly, many of our missing people are of a demographic that does not possess any types of higher-end electronics which would have tracking capabilities." Access to a signal or Wi-Fi and a power source is often required for tracking in some technologies. These can be limitations to tracking technologies being leveraged in police SAR work. Nevertheless, police SAR operations can use these tools to locate missing persons when possible and appropriate.

Project Lifesaver is one such tool, documented as "the premier search and rescue program operated internationally by public safety agencies" (Project Lifesaver, 2022) for persons at risk of going missing and wandering, notably those with cognitive disorders like Alzheimer's and dementia. It involves radio frequency (RF) tracking technologies that use radio waves to send and receive signal information between two devices to determine a person's location (Topfer, 2016). RF devices are provided for persons registered in the program and worn daily as an accessory or embedded in the individual's clothing, so there is no need to remember to activate or carry them (Mahoney & Mahoney, 2010). Ergo, as an individual would wear this at all times, they would always be trackable. Being part of Project Lifesaver requires registration in the program, so it is not available as an impromptu tool for use in police SAR work. Participant 2001 described Project Lifesaver and some limitations to its utility:

> It's basically tracking equipment based on radio frequency technology … When a person subscribes to that program, they put on a bracelet that looks almost like a watch. And if they're wearing that, then we should be able to track those people using that radio frequency machine, the equipment. Some limitations are the fact that you have to change the battery once a month. So, if that gets forgotten, then it stops transmitting. And the other challenge to that is that you have to get within 500 meters of the individual for the signal to be picked up on.

There are tracking tools that can be used in scenarios of people going missing without prior incident, notice, or registry to a program, such as GPS, proximity, or other radio location technologies. For example, GPS is a worldwide system that can identify a person's location using a transmitter that sends signals received by cell phones and mobile tracking tools to a network of geostationary telecommunications satellites (Topfer, 2016; Bulat et al., 2016). Due to this, GPS devices can typically locate a person in large areas or really anywhere in which a satellite signal can reach. However, any obstructions separating the connection between the satellite and receiver (i.e., cloud coverage, inclement weather) inhibit GPS's utility (Bulat et al., 2016). Some devices with GPS that can be accessed for locating a missing person include cell phones, vehicles, navigation systems, smartwatches, bike accessories like securing systems, and even hiking sticks (Makmanee, 2013). Regarding vehicle GPS tracking, Participant 27001 noted, "We would open up a GPS map by using what's called 'parked location,' click 'locate vehicle' and then it would show where their vehicle is with a dot on screen, sometimes an address too." Proximity technologies such as Bluetooth or radio location can be harnessed in SAR. Bluetooth uses Bluetooth Low Energy (BLE) to connect to devices wirelessly and transmit snippets of data to other devices through that connection. Each Bluetooth device typically has a unique signature and is, therefore, recognized as specific to that device and owner (Aging and Innovation Research Program, n.d.). An example of Bluetooth tracking technologies in our data is the Apple Airtag for iPhones, which officers said is especially useful in locating people in densely populated areas (e.g., urban environments).

5.2.9 Collaboration

All of these activities, tools, and technologies may be outsourced to or the responsibility of other police and non-police groups across Canada. In other words, collaboration is a tool used by police for SAR work. In fact, it is one of the most emphasized tools mentioned for locating missing persons. Because the capacity and tools to conduct SAR activities vary by service, it becomes a matter of pooling resources to complete operations and relying on the resources and personnel of other police services. Participant 1009 explained intra-agency collaboration:

> you could be sitting at home on the deck, having a beer, and you're four hours off work, and all of a sudden, the phone rings. Because we want to help out, we want to find more people. You could be working and not even be involved in the case. And then all of a sudden, you hear about it, and you call them and say, 'I hear you've got this going, if you need anything, let me know.' And you always offer that support and try and help out to find the person.

Participant 7007 offered an example of inter-agency collaboration as a tool: "Another organization who had not the experience that we have in the search component went to the location and said they searched it, so there's no way that that person is there. We go the following day with our plan in place. We start our search. We utilize our cadaver dogs. Lo and behold, guess what we find? We find the deceased missing person."

Non-police groups were emphasized as invaluable. Such partnerships introduce and offer expertise and human resources that the police may not have. For example, in Newfoundland, the Cougar Helicopters specializes in helicopter aerial SAR (Cougar, 2023); in Alberta, the volunteer Underwater Search Team specializes in diving and underwater SAR (The Underwater Search Team, 2022); and in Manitoba, the SAR Dog Association provides a "contingent of four-legged searchers" for ground and heavy urban searches (Search & Rescue Manitoba, 2011).

Beyond these specialized volunteer groups, the public (including the families and loved ones of the missing) can also be engaged as additional human resources to support and assist in the operation, typically fulfilling the role of Searchers and completing grid search activities with oversight from the Search Lead or Search Manager. The public is generally only introduced to large-scale SAR operations that need more boots-on-the-ground support. They would be organized by the leading Search Manager and overhead team, with the understanding that many would not be highly qualified or even experienced. For the operation's success, the leading Search Manager and the overhead team would supply any volunteers with information that is relevant to the incident, like up-to-date weather reports, designated areas, tasks to be completed, what to look out for, and any need-to-know case specifics.

5.3 Additional Work Relevant to the Operation

The following work also occurs while police undertake SAR action as a part of the broader police response to missing persons. These are interdependent with SAR, in that these tasks can impact SAR response and vice versa.

5.3.1 Concurrent Police Investigation

The leading Search Manager and overhead team are in constant communication with the Incident Commander and any other key personnel on the ground or in-agency (e.g., Missing Persons Unit), providing updates on the response's progress and results. For example, as SAR efforts are being conducted, an investigation tends to run concurrently. That is, "there is the search side, and then there's the investigative side, and they work together to find the missing person" (Participant 30002). Aside from the obvious reason of putting all the necessary resources toward locating individuals, parallel investigations occur to inform the SAR efforts. Participant 1007 said, "If we find out a piece of information that a person likes to attend a certain area, then that might affect how we deploy our people in the search." Participant 28001 noted that these concurrent responses could also be needed to explore and rule out the chances of foul play: "We have to stop to think about foul play. Why did that person call a missing person in that particular point in time? Did they actually have a hand in having them go missing? … You still need to keep that in the back of your head." Therefore, police SAR personnel engaged in the response are supported by other officers throughout the organization, like frontline patrol, who are conducting an array of investigative activities to gather "information which is integral to the search" (Participant 5005) and "to generate leads" (Participant 39001). During an operation, updates in and out of the response typically come from the command post via radio: "I'm always asking for communication from patrol. In the command post, you know, whoever's closest to the radio, it's usually … Whoever this is says like, 'Hey,' and then that patrol person says, 'Yeah, command to whomever, can we get an update here?'" (Participant 23001).

Investigative avenues can include (yet are not limited to) missing persons appeals, cell phone and other GPS location pings (e.g., registries like Project Lifesaver), conducting and following up on interviews with friends/acquaintances and family, street or door-to-door canvassing, looking for video footage, garnering the individual's social media information and recent activity (e.g., from Facebook, Instagram,

Snapchat), and retrieving financial records. Media officers can be involved in putting out a missing persons appeal via news outlets and police social media pages, and liaising with the media to keep them updated on the SAR operation. "It just gives you that many more eyes to help locate this missing person," Participant 13001 said about the use of missing persons appeals, "I can't give you a number of how many times that we've received information that solved it, that has led to the actual successful locating the missing person. It's been many." As another example, financial records can help offer locational information, like the PLS or PLK:

> We tap into our Financial Crime Unit because someone goes missing, and all of a sudden, you do a financial check, and you find out they bank at [bank name redacted], you contact their corporate security, you explain to them circumstances – they're suicidal, there's issues, and there is information they're going to harm themselves or someone else. All of a sudden, they get back to you in 20 minutes and say, 'Yeah, so-and-so just use the ATM at [street name redacted] street at the [bank name redacted].' It's another tool that you can use. (Participant 41002)

The investigation activities above are not strictly limited to officers outside of SAR work—police SAR personnel may also ping a cell phone, canvass door to door, interview families and loved ones, and request financial records. The dividing line between investigations and SAR is pretty transparent, or at least blurred, because these types of responses are interdependent. The SAR mission is reliant on information from investigation-related activities and vice versa. Therefore, while some officers view these as separate sides of the same coin (police response to missing persons), they are one of the same in practice. All in all, the investigation does not drop off immediately when SAR action is undertaken. It can be vital that both types of efforts continue.

5.3.2 *Communication with Families and Loved Ones and the Media*

The family and loved ones of the missing are also kept informed about any SAR developments, often by the leading Search Manager or a SAR team member appointed as the family liaison. This person may instead be in-agency, like the Missing Persons Coordinator, who would receive updates from the SAR personnel conducting the response and communicate these outward. Whenever possible, officers expressed that it is best to have just one person assigned as the liaison to ensure the consistency and continuity of updates. It could be the case that the family and loved ones are on-site and helping in the operation (e.g., as Searchers), so they are receiving in-the-moment updates from the SAR team this way. Finally, the media are also sometimes informed about any developments in the case and the SAR response through briefings, typically conducted by a media relations police officer, the leading Search Manager, or Incident Commander.

References

Aging and Innovation Research Program. (n.d.). *Locator devices for people at risk of going missing*. Retrieved from https://uwaterloo.ca/aging-innovation-research-program/locator-devices

Bulat, T., Kerrigan, M. V., Rowe, M., Kearns, W., Craighead, J. D., & Ramaiah, P. (2016). Field evaluations of tracking/locating technologies for prevention of missing incidents. *American Journal of Alzheimer's Disease & Other Dementias, 31*(6), 474–480.

Cai, C., Chen, J., Yan, Q., Liu, F., & Zhou, R. (2022). A prior information-based coverage path planner for underwater search and rescue using autonomous underwater vehicle (AUV) with side-scan sonar. *IET Radar, Sonar & Navigation, 16*(7), 1225–1239.

Caplan, J. M. (2014). *Risk terrain modeling for strategic and tactical action*. Crime Mapping and Analysis News, A Police Foundation Publication.

Cougar. (2023). *Cougar helicopters search & rescue*. Retrieved from https://www.cougar.ca/what-we-do.html

CTV News. (2014). *RCMP officer showcases drone technology on Katie Couric show*. Retrieved from https://saskatoon.ctvnews.ca/rcmp-officer-showcases-drone-technology-on-katie-couric-show-1.1651127?cache=pawumraq

Custers, B. (2012). Technology in policing: Experiences, obstacles and police needs. *Computer Law & Security Review, 28*(1), 62–68.

Denver, M., Perez, J., & Aguirre, B. E. (2007). Local search and rescue teams in the United States. *Disaster Prevention and Management, 16*(4), 503–512.

Ericson, R. V., & Shearing, C. D. (1986). The scientification of police work. In *The knowledge society: The growing impact of scientific knowledge on social relations* (pp. 129–159). Dordrecht: Springer Netherlands.

Fatih, T., & Bekir, C. (2015). Police use of technology to fight against crime. *European Scientific Journal, 11*(10), 286–296.

Ferguson, L., & Soave, V. (2021). #missing to #found: Exploring police twitter use for missing persons investigations. *Police Practice and Research, 22*(1), 869–885.

Ferguson, L., Gaub, J. E., & Huey, L. (2021). Exploring the roles and function of police search and rescue teams in Canadian agencies. *Policing: A Journal of Policy and Practice, 15*(3), 1701–1712.

Ferworn, A., Sadeghian, A., Barnum, K., Rahnama, H., Pham, H., Erickson, C., et al. (2006). Urban search and rescue with canine augmentation technology. In *Proceedings 2006 IEEE/SMC international conference* (pp. 334–338).

Fish, J. P., & Carr, H. A. (1990). *Sound underwater images: a guide to the generation and interpretation of side scan sonar data*. Retrieved from https://cir.nii.ac.jp/crid/1130000794814135296

Guinness World Book of Records. (2023). *First life saved by a search and rescue drone*. Retrieved from https://www.guinnessworldrecords.com/world-records/397609-first-life-saved-by-a-search-and-rescue-drone

Han, S., Chon, S., Kim, J., Seo, J., Shin, D. G., Park, S., et al. (2022). Snake robot gripper module for search and rescue in narrow spaces. *IEEE Robotics and Automation Letters, 7*(2), 1667–1673.

Kardasz, P., Doskocz, J., Hejduk, M., Wiejkut, P., & Zarzycki, H. (2016). Drones and possibilities of their using. *Journal of Civil and Environmental Engineering, 6*(3), 1–7.

Layton, J., & Gleim, S. (2023). *How search-and-rescue dogs work*. Retrieved from https://animals.howstuffworks.com/animal-facts/sar-dog2.htm

Lindqvist, B., Karlsson, S., Koval, A., Tevetzidis, I., Haluška, J., Kanellakis, C., et al. (2022). Multimodality robotic systems: Integrated combined legged-aerial mobility for subterranean search-and-rescue. *Robotics and Autonomous Systems, 154*, 104134.

Logan, N. (2016). *How police are using drones in the search for Chase Martens and other missing people*. Retrieved from https://globalnews.ca/news/2601141/how-police-are-using-drones-in-the-search-for-chase-martens-and-other-missing-people/

Mahoney, E. L., & Mahoney, D. F. (2010). Acceptance of wearable technology by people with Alzheimer's disease: Issues and accommodations. *American Journal of Alzheimer's Disease & Other Dementias, 25*(6), 527–531.

Makmanee, T. (2013). *From smartphone GPS bike mounts to GPS walking sticks*. Retrieved from https://www.trendhunter.com/slideshow/modern-gps-devices

Pensieri, M. G., Garau, M., & Barone, P. M. (2020). Drones as an integral part of remote sensing technologies to help missing people. *Drones, 4*(2), 15.

Półka, M., Ptak, S., & Kuziora, Ł. (2017). The use of UAV's for search and rescue operations. *Procedia Engineering, 192*, 748–752.

Project Lifesaver. (2022). *About project lifesaver*. Retrieved from https://projectlifesaver.org/

Public Safety Canada. (2013). *Quadrennial search and rescue review*. Retrieved from https://www.publicsafety.gc.ca/cnt/rsrcs/pblctns/archive-nss-qdrnnl-rvw/archive-nss-qdrnnl-rvw-en.pdf

Ribeiro, C., Ferworn, A., Denko, M., Tran, J., & Mawson, C. (2008). Wireless estimation of canine pose for search and rescue. In *2008 IEEE International Conference* (pp. 1–6).

Ritzer, G. (1993). *The McDonaldization of Society*. Thousand Oaks, CA: Pine Forge Press.

Schultz, J. J., Healy, C. A., Parker, K., & Lowers, B. (2013). Detecting submerged objects: The application of side scan sonar to forensic contexts. *Forensic Science International, 231*(1–3), 306–316.

Search & Rescue Manitoba. (2011). *Search and Rescue Manitoba Volunteer Association*. Retrieved from http://www.searchandrescuevolunteer.ca/

Silvagni, M., Tonoli, A., Zenerino, E., & Chiaberge, M. (2017). Multipurpose UAV for search and rescue operations in mountain avalanche events. *Geomatics, Natural Hazards and Risk, 8*(1), 18–33.

Sparkes, J. (2021). *Check Your Sources – What the Public Needs to Know About Missing Persons Data*. Retrieved from https://www.missingpersonsresearchhub.com/post/check-your-sources-what-the-public-needs-to-know-about-missing-persons-data

Stuart, D. R. (2013). *Social media: Establishing criteria for law enforcement use*. Retrieved from http://www.fbi.gov/stats-services/publications/law-enforcement-bulletin/2013/february/social-media-establishing-criteria-for-lawenforcement-use

The Underwater Search Team. (2022). *The Underwater Search Team*. Retrieved from https://underwatersearchteam.com/

Topfer, L. A. (2016). *GPS locator devices for people with dementia*. Retrieved from https://europepmc.org/article/nbk/nbk391026

Visser, J. T., & Campbell, A. F. R. (2014). New Zealand land search and rescue operations. *Wilderness & Environmental Medicine, 25*(4), 401–408.

Wang, J. (2003). A game engine based simulation of the NIST urban search and rescue arenas. In *Proceedings of the 2003 winter simulation conference, 2003* (Vol. 1, pp. 1039–1045). IEEE. Retrieved from https://ieeexplore.ieee.org/abstract/document/1261528/

Weidlich, J. (2013). *Aerial drone locates Sask. Man injured in rollover crash*. Retrieved from: https://www.cbc.ca/news/canada/saskatchewan/aerial-drone-locates-sask-man-injured-in-rollover-crash-1.1398942

Wojtusiak, J., & Nia, R. M. (2021). Location prediction using GPS trackers: Can machine learning help locate the missing people with dementia? *Internet of Things, 13*, 100035.

Chapter 6
The Events After Police Search and Rescue Response

6.1 What Is a "Successful" Search and Rescue Operation?

Maple Ridge, British Columbia (June 2023) 16-year-old Esther Wang went missing while hiking with a small group of teenagers along the East Canyon trail in Golden Ears Provincial Park (Gouda, 2023). The group stopped briefly at Steve's Lookout and then resumed their hike. Some 15 minutes later, the Group Leader realized one hiker was missing. They quickly set about to look for Esther before flagging down a Park Ranger, who called the police (Reilly, 2023).

Police quickly engaged the local volunteer search and rescue (SAR) team, who knew how difficult the park terrain was. They searched through the night (Canadian Press, 2023). Attempts to "ping" Esther's cell phone were unsuccessful because of the remote location. Instead, rescuers were "very much reliant … on boots on the ground" (Corporal Julie Klaussener, cited in McSheffrey, 2023). By the morning of the second day Esther had been missing, SAR teams from across Vancouver's Lower Mainland had joined the effort, a helicopter and drone were attempting an aerial search, and the police had some 45 different resources deployed (Canadian Press, 2023). Around 54 hours after she had first disappeared, Esther walked out of the trail, alive and well (Reilly, 2023).

"Successful" resolution of missing persons cases in police SAR is locating the individual. Participant 1002 explained, "'Success' to a Searcher is we find the person. No matter what the state is, we find them … For the family, for that closure, or for that, 'oh my gosh, thank goodness you found my loved one,' our objective is to find the individual, whatever the condition is, that's the success. If we don't, then we didn't have success." Esther appearing out of the woods meant the SAR operation was successful. But, the police's work does not end here. Various activities occur after the response, ranging from operational debriefings to report writing to criminal investigations to referrals to supports and services. This chapter dives into the events

L. Ferguson, L. Huey, *Police Search and Rescue Response to Lost and Missing Persons*, SpringerBriefs in Criminology,
https://doi.org/10.1007/978-3-031-44077-9_6

that transpire after a police SAR response, shedding light on the post-operations phase and the trajectories for resolved and unresolved cases thereafter.

6.2 Post-operation Activities

6.2.1 Suspension or Termination of the Operation

Suspension or termination occurs when a response is called off temporarily or permanently. As we explain below, SAR efforts may cease because the evaluation or progress of the response by the Incident Commander, leading Search Manager, and/or overhead team urges it. SAR efforts may also be suspended or terminated if the missing person or their remains are located, they return their own volition like Esther Wang, resources have been depleted, or the report is deemed unfounded.

If reasonable SAR efforts have been made without locating the missing person, and there is no sound information or leads to continue, police may suspend active SAR efforts temporarily. When there are no credible leads, it becomes challenging to determine the areas where the individual may be located, and SAR action can become unfocused and less effective. These issues cannot be resolved by simply persevering. Pausing SAR action is a difficult but strategic decision to gain the opportunity to regroup, gather additional case information (e.g., from witnesses or the public), and consider alternative response avenues that may generate new leads, clues, or search areas. By suspending the response, expending resources on tenuous or unproductive SAR efforts is avoided, and the focus is shifted to obtaining credible information to guide future action. Operations may also be paused due to extreme weather or environmental factors (e.g., snow blizzards, severe storms, water levels), making it too hazardous to continue or impossible to ground pound and operate equipment; this entails waiting for more favorable conditions, reducing the risk to personnel and improving equipment utility. The suspension is continually reassessed, and once the conditions subside and if deemed safe, SAR activities resume.

An operation may be terminated when all possible efforts have been exhausted, and there is no reasonable expectation of finding the missing person. This decision is typically based on a careful evaluation of available information and the operation's progress, as well as expert advice from SAR personnel. Terminating the response involves demobilizing resources and concluding the operation. This process can be a structured deactivation effort by systematically calling off resources and pulling in equipment one by one or a broad radio message to all Searchers to return to the command post. The former typically occurs in larger-scale responses and the latter in smaller operations. Personnel are thus pulled out of active SAR efforts and notified of the decision to suspend or terminate the mission. As a part of this, the leading Search Manager and the overhead team must account for police and non-police resources allocated to the response. Sometimes sign-out sheets for volunteers and other personnel are utilized to aid in resource management. Equipment must be turned in, checked, and returned to the appropriate personnel or group.

An operational debrief or review of the incident may then occur, which is discussed in the next section. Other actions include deactivating the command center and ensuring the search area is left clear. Note that if the SAR operation is suspended, the command post remains operational so information can still filter in, and there is a centralized place to evaluate and conduct ongoing and future response efforts. Some clean-up activities include taking down tents and tables, packing away technology such as laptops and handheld tracker devices, and saving and storing any documentation that occurred (e.g., filing clue logs, saving Global Positioning System (GPS) maps to computer files). Any tape cordoning off areas, clue markers, and other materials in-field must be documented, removed from the search area, and packed away. All termination activities are completed carefully and thoughtfully, keeping in mind that the same people and equipment could be called out to conduct a SAR operation at any time, even seconds after one concludes. Police SAR teams tend to handle termination as though they are packing their equipment and resources for the next response.

The suspension or termination of a SAR operation is not giving up on the missing person even though they have not been located. Rather, it reflects a transition to a different phase where the focus shifts from SAR action to other response activities like scouring for leads, following up with the reportee and witnesses, looking for video surveillance, and retrieving financial records. Police continue to gather information, investigate, and engage in ongoing efforts. These phases are discussed in the upcoming section on case trajectories. Finally, SAR operations may be wound down if other policing responsibilities crop up that take priority and require resources. In situations where multiple incidents or emergencies occur at once, police need to prioritize their allocation of limited resources. When a more pressing situation requires immediate attention, personnel and equipment resources may be redirected to address it. This decision is based on the assessment of the level of risk and urgency of each incident, with the most emergency situation being prioritized.

6.2.2 *Debriefings*

6.2.2.1 Operational Debriefings

Operational debriefings are aimed at gathering and sharing experiences and information, assessing the mission, and identifying learnings for future responses. Participant 5005 said these capture "lessons learned, because it doesn't matter how well you do, there are always things to be learned … We always like to do debriefs and, 'How can we do this better? How can we improve this?'" Debriefings may occur on-scene when the mission concludes or shortly after when police are back in the agency. The former helps gather in-the-moment reflections and insights because all personnel are still in the search area and to account for all equipment and people. The latter helps with establishing police-specific learnings for improving this work. Depending upon the incident, its scale, and the number of personnel, these can happen with just the leading Search Manager and overhead team or with all police and non-police who remain on-scene.

Some police only conduct operational debriefings after larger-scale operations, high-profile cases (e.g., those that grabbed the public's and media's attention), and missions that were unsuccessful. "We usually do a debriefing when there's been negative outcomes. If the person is succumbed to the circumstances, we like to have a debriefing just to understand where we can improve" (Participant 22001). Debriefings only occurring in these select scenarios are because such incidents are outside of more routine SAR operations, involve greater complexity, scale, resources, multi-group coordination, and safety and risk concerns, and have more potential for communication gaps, coordination challenges, and logistical issues that necessitate debriefing.

Operational debriefings are generally lessons-focused and systems-focused to be useful and constructive. Being lessons-focused means paying attention to learning and improvement opportunities and exploring what went well and could be improved. Participant 1010 detailed, "This is sitting down with everybody that went there, and you walk through—'All right, the call came in at this time, and you were the first person there, what did you do?', 'Oh, I did this, this, this, and this.' And then your three points that you thought went well, your three points that didn't go well." Systems-focused means assessing the operation from the perspective of the overall incident versus paying attention to individual performance "to avoid blame culture and to have a more comprehensive review" (Participant 4003).

However, there is no established after-action review system. Debriefings occur ad hoc and are agency- and case-dependent. Some police services do not conduct these at all. They also hinge on the personnel involved in the response, especially the overhead team and Search Manager as these roles are primarily responsible for initiating and organizing debriefings and hold decision-making power as to if these happen. In some agencies, the Missing Persons Coordinator or Missing Persons Unit might also request a debrief with the police SAR team. However, as Participant 7003 said, "A dedicated after-action review system would be extremely beneficial, not just for the search management side of things but for everyone involved in it, from the initial stages right through to the end." This is because debriefings can be useful for future trainings, lessons learned, and case studies. For instance, Search Coordinators, who are responsible for the internal SAR program, utilize debriefings by "recording all those and then putting out lessons learned documents. So, even if only one person reads it, it might help them down the road … the more we do that, the better we get at what we do" (Participant 3002).

6.2.2.2 Debriefings with Missing People

Another type of debriefing is interviewing missing persons after they are located. In the literature, these have been termed *return home interviews* and *return support discussions* (e.g., Shalev et al., 2009; Ferguson & Sidebottom, 2022). The primary reasons for these are to capture "as much detail as possible on the activities and whereabouts of the missing person during their absence, as well as the reason for them going missing" (Participant 5003). They can also provide the chance to record information that may be valuable if the person goes missing again, such as locations frequented or known associates. These are typically short, informal, and occur face-to-face to verify the individual's safety and well-being and develop rapport:

> We physically have to have a face-to-face interview with anybody who is now found … Especially when it comes to youth, we have to make sure of that because a lot of times they can be vulnerable to be recruited into human trafficking and escort services and stuff like that, so we'd have to attend the house and then build a rapport with the youth and then hopefully they would feel comfortable to give you some information. (Participant 2007)

Other chief objectives are to uncover if the missing person experienced anything while missing (e.g., harm, emotional turmoil, exposure to the elements) that requires attention and make recommendations to supports and services. During this, police may offer resource information and referrals for counseling, medical care, or other services. As an example, if the individual has dementia, Participant 7008 explained, "We have to provide information to the family or loved one and the missing person about the Vulnerable Person Registry and Project Lifesaver to try to prevent future incidents and ensure their continued safety and well-being." In this way, these debriefings can mark an important step toward support for the individual and their families and loved ones.

Beyond documenting the individual's account and experiences, debriefings allow the police to speak to people about ways of contacting the police if they go missing again. This is a rapport- and relationship-building exercise for hopefully reducing the risk of future missing events. Officers detailed that they provide their cell phone numbers, emails, and agency contact details to located persons and their families and loved ones. Participant 9001 explained that, after rapport is developed through these discussions, people "have no problem sending a text like, 'Yeah, I'm not going home,' or, 'I'm not at so and so's,' or, 'I'm scared I'm going to get beat up, so I'm going to stay at a friend's place.' And that solves the file." Participant 1010 further said that debriefings with located persons "develop a really good rapport with people … If they text us, 'No, I'm not missing. I'm just not going home right now' … it could easily be solved with just a text message from someone that they know." Although police sometimes have to physically see the person to close the report and verify their identity and well-being. However, there are many ways for this to occur (as noted above, such as text messages), and once their identity and well-being are verified, police reach their authority limit for looking for the person. As Participant 4006 explained in relation to capable adults that go missing, "It is important for people to understand that if we have verified a person's identity and well-being, we have absolutely no authority to continue looking for them and/or to insist that they meet with us in person—they don't have to, and many people don't want to." Debriefings with missing people occur in the manner in which the individual allows it and is appropriate for the case.

6.2.2.3 Debriefings with Families, Loved Ones, and the Public

Debriefings with families and loved ones of the missing, and sometimes the public in the case of high-profile incidents, are conducted by the officer tasked with being the liaison. In this context, debriefings refer to continued communication about the case and any updates. Their exact format and structure vary depending on the case circumstances; however, the general components are information sharing, addressing questions and concerns, and providing support. Police may conduct these via phone calls, in-person visits, email, and/or through media channels and press releases. In these sessions, police may share details about the operation, including the strategies employed, areas covered, challenges faced, and any significant findings. These debriefings allow families and loved ones and the public to ask any questions, have their concerns addressed, and understand the case's next steps. If and while cases remain unresolved and open files, debriefings may continue ad hoc as much or as little as the families and loved ones would like and if there are any case updates (e.g., new leads or information comes to light). However, some officers also noted that these debriefings do not occur often enough as it is an informal and arbitrary task.

6.2.3 Incident Recording

Incident recording is a central aspect of the police role and function, and, as such, there is a body of scholarship dedicated to investigating police-recorded data and police knowledge work and management activities (see Ericson, 1982; Luen & Al-Hawamdeh, 2001; Giacomantonio, 2015). For example, studies have observed that police spend a significant portion of their on-duty hours completing paperwork, forms, and reports rather than their patrol and response duties (Ericson, 1982; Malm et al., 2005; Brodeur & Dupont, 2006; Huey et al., 2022a). One of the major goals of police incident recording and data processes is to create useful information to achieve organizational mandates (Huey et al., 2022b). Other reasons include seeking increased efficiencies, understanding operational activities and performance, directing police activities, and fulfilling liability and audit requirements (Brimicombe, 2016; Giacomantonio, 2015; Huey et al., 2022b).

Police SAR work involves such tasks, too, like filling out paperwork, creating files, folders, databases, and spreadsheets, and writing reports. Police complete these various documentation activities for recording the operation and internal uses such as training and skill development, tactical and strategic planning, policy and procedure development, and analytical work.

> Our Search Coordinator, he has a computer file where it's a folder that has all of our Level 1 SAR that are in that folder from each year … he's had it going for, I think, about three or four years now. He's been keeping track because what happens is with your different variety of experiences that your Search Managers have, like we have some that have only been Search Managers for a year or two, and we have others who have been doing it for ten plus years like myself. So, you have a lot of different experience to what you've done. It's good because they can go into that file and see what was used, techniques maybe that they've never done before, and that makes them better at what they do. (Participant 11002)

In line with other crime- and social-related incidents, police SAR personnel are tasked with reporting an account of the incident to log an official record of it (Giacomantonio, 2015). This log might be reviewed by various police personnel (e.g., the Missing Persons Coordinator, Missing Persons Unit personnel, Duty Inspector, on-duty supervisor, and Incident Commander) for quality assurance purposes and to ensure it reflects the response activities. If information is missed in this systematized input or the file is otherwise not correctly logged (e.g., inaccurate or missing demographic information), it may be caught by these personnel who review submitted reports as a part of the chain of information processing (Giacomantonio, 2015). That said, completing and reviewing the report is often just the responsibility of the officer(s) who conducted the SAR action.

A mission may also be recorded as a *case study*. These tend to contain detailed descriptions of the missing person (e.g., age, sex/gender, physical features like height) and the operation, such as its context, challenges, response strategies, and outcomes. Incident descriptions, including the location, date, time, and circumstances surrounding the missing person event, are regular features of case studies. Extracted from the Action Plan established in the planning and operational periods, the objectives and scope of the SAR operation may be included too. Developing SAR case studies is not a formalized duty but a task some personnel take on to serve as a resource for training, planning, and improving future responses. Participant 1002 explained that their agency "does case studies because we want to be able to say, 'OK, what worked, what didn't work, what was a hindrance, what was not a hit?'" The selection of incidents turned into case studies is typically that of SAR missions that were tricky, unique, complex, and/or had crucial lessons learned. As a part of the internal program maintenance, the Search Coordinator may select which cases to utilize as case studies, or it may be a collective decision made among police SAR personnel. The Search Coordinator is also commonly responsible for the actual creation of these case studies.

Because case studies highlight successful approaches, strategies, and techniques employed in past operations, they hold a record of the methods that yielded positive outcomes to serve as benchmarks for future operations. As in, they feature the agency's internal best practices across a range of scenarios. Case studies also have details on unsuccessful components of responses. These provide a record of the challenging factors or any operational failures. Participant 1008 noted that these give SAR teams the opportunity to "identify areas for improvement and implement corrective measures to address our potential shortcomings." They are also leveraged as training resources for SAR personnel, providing real-life learning and skill development scenarios encountered in previous operations to apply knowledge in a practical context.

6.2.4 Data Recording, Storing, and Management

Police gather a range of data before, during, and after an operation. As noted in earlier chapters, part of the planning and operational phases is setting up and completing various documentation processes to capture data. Data can also come from sources outside of what derives from a mission, such as investigative efforts or the public submitting leads and information. Instances of data gathered over the life of an operation include reportee and witness statements, information about the missing person, SAR task reports and team logs, clue logs, digital maps, communication records, and resource records. For example, after an operation, detailed reports are completed and submitted by police personnel in an agency's Record Management System (RMS) that outline the case's key aspects, including a synopsis of the service call, the reason for SAR action, the sequence of response events, actions taken, and mission outcomes. Reports may also include photographs, maps, or other visual aids. Moreover, any relevant evidence (e.g., personal belongings found during the SAR operation) is carefully preserved and recorded following established protocols for each police agency.

Data may be stored in a centralized database or specialized database within the relevant unit with SAR responsibilities (e.g., Public Order Unit), or both, depending on the specific protocols in each agency. One officer explained that beyond their agency-wide RMS, they also maintain a specialized database entitled *SAR Docs*, "S-A-R. Search and rescue docs or documents, which is like Excel spreadsheets that accompany the operation" (Participant 1009). Collected data are documented and recorded in a secure and accessible system, which varies by service.

6.3 Post-operation Case Trajectories

What happens to the file once a SAR response is concluded? The trajectories of a case depend on the incident specifics, available evidence, and outcome of the SAR operation. The main paths are case clearance and case transfer or reassignment. Case clearance occurs when files are concluded, whereas case transfer or reassignment is relevant to files that remain open despite SAR efforts.

6.3.1 Case Clearance

Case clearance refers to the closure of a missing person incident. It signifies that police have taken the necessary actions to arrive at a resolution (located or established their identity and well-being) and have determined the circumstances surrounding the individual's disappearance. There are two main ways in which clearing missing persons cases occurs. One is that the individual or their remains are located by way of police response, community efforts, self-reporting or returning of their own volition, or any other ways in which an individual becomes no longer missing. This scenario does not always mean an entirely positive outcome. Tragically, some missing persons are found deceased, resulting from various factors, including accidents, harm, exposure to the elements, or natural causes. If the cause and circumstances of the individual's death are determined, and no additional efforts are required of the police, the case can be cleared. But, as we discuss in the next section, a deceased missing person may need further police investigation and follow-up to ensure a thorough understanding of the events surrounding the death before the case is cleared.

The second route occurs when it is determined that the individual was not actually missing, called an *unfounded report*. This could be due to miscommunication or misunderstanding regarding an individual's whereabouts, false reporting, or insufficient evidence that a person is actually missing. Miscommunication or misunderstanding can happen for various reasons that contribute to the misinterpretation of a person's absence, such as the individual being away on vacation, their cell phone battery dying so they lose contact with their social network, or even being late for curfew. False reporting incidents can and do occur too. An officer provided the example of a reportee reporting an individual missing because the reportee was owed money, and thus the reportee wanted to locate them to get money back but could not find them—which does not constitute a missing persons incident.

Without substantial or reliable evidence suggesting a person is missing, it becomes challenging for police to continue treating the file as an active missing persons case. For police to investigate an incident, there must be grounds to do so. Sometimes, individuals may voluntarily go out of contact or be absent without informing others. And in Canada, it is not a crime (i.e., not an offense under the Criminal Code) for capable adults to do so; they can go missing without criminal sanctions (Ferguson, 2022). If there is no or insufficient evidence of a disappearance, or foul play or imminent danger, police may conclude that the person's absence is not indicative of a missing persons situation. A case thus may be cleared if it involves a capable adult that chose to disconnect from their social network or take off. This is not the case for vulnerable persons, as laws prohibit them from being unaccompanied or absent from their parent, guardian, or place of safety as a protection measure. For instance, children and youth that go missing will not be subject to criminal sanctions; however, they can be apprehended by the police without a warrant in certain circumstances (e.g., imminent danger) and if they are under the age of protection set out in the jurisdiction's legislation (i.e., under 16 years old) and returned to their parent or caregiver (e.g., see Child, Family and Community Service Act). Cases being cleared because it is deemed that the individual is not missing carefully evaluate the risk or vulnerability factors related to the incident and the relevant local legislation (e.g., a regional *Missing Persons Act*) that guides the determination of who is missing and what circumstances are captured as missing incidents.

6.3.2 Case Transfer or Reassignment

If police are unable to locate the missing person alive or deceased through SAR action, the case may get transferred to another area of policing for further investigation, file review, and planning the next investigative steps:

> What happens is if we have a missing person file, and we as a search management team are not able to locate that individual, then what happens is that gets bumped over … All missing people cases get bumped over to our Major Crimes section. The Major Crimes section has a Missing Persons Coordinator. That Missing Persons Coordinator gets the files that are reviewed by the Major Crimes office, and then they will continue with follow-ups relating to the missing person until they're located, or someone would be tasked with that file if the individual has not been located and there's some suspect of issues like high-risk lifestyle, evidence that there's something to suggest that potentially they were abducted or could be in a relationship where there's potential they've been harm … Something that would jump out to the Major Crimes section. (Participant 1011)

These files would remain with this other policing area as long as they remain open. As time passes and investigative avenues and techniques dry up, open files become what is more widely known as *cold cases* (also *historical* or *long-term cases*). Cold cases are missing persons files in which "everything has been done that could be done" (Participant 4001), but there are "no other investigative tactics to use and all types of oversight and review find the same that there's nothing more that can be done in that moment" (Participant 3004) (in Bennett & Ferguson, 2022).

No dedicated system, guidelines, or framework exists for cold/long-term files across the nation (Bennett & Ferguson, 2022). Indeed, there are no police Cold Case Units for missing persons in Canada. As such, officers explained that unresolved cases may end up "falling through the cracks" or receiving "little follow-up attention" (Participant 7007) (Bennett & Ferguson, 2022). This means that unresolved cases are the responsibility of various personnel or units throughout the policing system. Some police organizations manage these cases under Missing Persons Units, Historical Case Detectives, or Missing Persons Coordinators. Others instead keep the case with general duty investigators to be responded to as one of their additional duties or "off the corner of someone's desk" (Participant 4003) (Bennett & Ferguson, 2022). If and when unresolved missing persons cases become resolved in the future, they would then be cleared and the files closed.

The case may also be transferred if foul play is suspected and/or the person is located deceased, and more efforts need to be taken to understand the cause and circumstances of their death. To complete such work, the file is moved to another area of policing that is most suitable for the case investigation. Participant 1005 stated, "Oftentimes, if there's foul play or things of that nature, then a Major Crime section is involved, and it becomes their investigation." These are typically major crimes, criminal investigations, or homicide divisions, especially if the causes are suspected to be linked to criminality. Further investigation and other police efforts will look to establish the cause of death, determine the circumstances leading to and surrounding their death, rule out or identify potential criminal activity, gather evidence as potentially necessary for legal proceedings, and provide conclusion to the family and loved ones.

The final case trajectory is that of case reassignment. Cases may be reassigned to another agency due to jurisdictional boundaries. If a case is discovered to fall outside the jurisdiction of the initial responding police service, it may be necessary to reassign the case to the appropriate agency with jurisdiction in the location where the incident occurred. This is because different police agencies have specific legal powers and authority within defined regional boundaries to handle the case and carry out necessary law enforcement activities. Further, case reassignment ensures that the agency with knowledge of local laws, resources, and community dynamics takes the lead in the investigation. It also means that the queue of cases at the initial agency is not being held up. Then, each agency can focus its efforts and allocate resources to the cases within its jurisdiction. Lastly, especially for unsuccessful SAR operations, ensuring appropriate agency assignment means that the investigation will be held in the jurisdiction where the person's remains will most likely be eventually found. If case reassignment is to occur, the initial responding agency would connect with the service with jurisdiction, reassign the file, and transfer its information. The incident is then cleared from the initial agency's response queue.

6.4 Impacts on Police Work

"It could be time constraints, it could be resource availability, it could be money, it could be any number of factors" (Participant 1003)—there are many reasons an operation may not be successful. This section explains the common challenges and successes related to police SAR work to offer context on what can impact the outcomes of an operation. One or several of these factors will be present in every police SAR response.

6.4.1 Challenges

6.4.1.1 Weather and Temperature

While police can monitor weather forecasts and make decisions based on available weather information, they contend with the unpredictability and variability of the weather and temperature. Adverse weather conditions can create operational limitations, including the inability to use particular SAR equipment, deploy personnel, or access search areas. For example, in the very cold, batteries discharge more quickly than in moderate or warm conditions, shortening the operational time of electronic devices with batteries, such as GPS units, radios, and wearable headlamps. Hence, reducing the amount of time police have to conduct their missions. When exposed to extreme heat, the components of radios, drones, and thermal imaging cameras can reach critical temperatures, causing them to shut down to prevent damage, disrupting communication, aerial reconnaissance, and the ability to detect heat signatures during SAR missions. Even what may be regarded as "normal" weather conditions can impact SAR operations. To illustrate, if police dogs are being utilized, the direction and speed of the wind can affect their detection of scent. If the wind changes directions, gusts, or blows hard, scents can be carried off the path of the missing person before getting to the dog's nose, and so the dog may be unable to follow a scent. This may impact delays in the operation or red herrings (i.e., following scent paths in the wrong direction). Beyond operational limitations, weather and temperature can also affect evidence and leads. As Participant 1007 said, "If it's very nasty outside—let's say heavy rain makes it difficult to see, makes it difficult to pick up sound." Rain can wash tracks and clues away. Blizzarding snow conditions and fog can make it tough to find any signs of missing persons due to low visibility and reach people due to reduced abilities to track and follow clues as to their whereabouts.

The climate also creates challenges for the people involved in the incident—the first responders and missing persons. The bitter cold and heat stress can affect SAR personnel's safety, performance, and endurance; "Extreme cold and heavy rain burns out your searchers" (Participant 13002). In these scenarios, police take additional precautions and provisions to ensure their well-being, like adding more break times and Searcher turnovers, reducing search zone sizes, or slowing down the operation. Further, Participant 1004 stressed, "Weather also heightens the risk factors when you're dealing with an individual who is lost or missing," generating questions such as "What are they wearing? Are they dressed for the conditions? You know you can be dressed in a warm parka, but if it's −35°, it doesn't matter … If you're out there for more than three hours, you're going to be freezing." Extreme temperatures can affect the survival chances of missing persons, especially if the individual is not suitably dressed for the weather. Put another way, climate can impact the police's concerns about the person's risk or vulnerability. In the cold, individuals who are not adequately prepared or protected, e.g., with appropriate clothing, may be at risk of hypothermia, frostbite, or other cold-related injuries. On the other hand, extreme heat can lead to dehydration, heat exhaustion, or heatstroke, particularly if the missing person is exposed to high temperatures for an extended period without access to water, shade, or shelter. Missing persons' vulnerability to adverse weather conditions can pose a pressing threat to their survival and well-being. Weather and temperature elevate the urgency associated with an incident, which impacts police SAR work (as we have discussed previously; e.g., the resources assigned, types of tasks taken on). Altogether, these factors can affect the operation, its equipment, the personnel tasked with locating missing people, and the missing people.

6.4.1.2 Terrain

> Terrain is another challenging factor. People don't think about this a lot. We get a lot of SAR in the area of the parks and the river, and that is a significant area that you can't … even sending a big team of people into an area, the probability of locating someone in a giant, grassy, thick, bushy area is really low. So even when you deploy police in the right area, you may be missing them. (Participant 1006)

Across Canada, the nature of the terrain police conduct SAR operations throughout can vary widely, including mountains, forests, water bodies, and urban areas. Starting with urban environments, the presence of buildings, crowded streets, and complex infrastructure can add complication to police SAR, as first mentioned in Chap. 4. Numerous buildings and structures can make narrowing the search area difficult. Visibility and access for SAR teams can be inhibited by tall buildings, street networks, and crowded areas obstructing the line of sight and making it challenging to spot the missing person or obtain visual clues. Limited visibility can also hamper aerial urban SAR efforts due to building structures or confined airspace. Urban environments can also make it particularly tricky to manage search areas, and avoiding clue disturbance and area contamination can be unfeasible.

Dense forests and wilderness areas pose challenges to navigation, visibility, Searcher coverage, and safety. The wilderness is often characterized by vast and unforgiving landscapes, such as rugged terrains or remote mountainous regions. Navigating these areas can be grueling and dangerous for SAR personnel, with limited or non-existent trails, dense vegetation, and rough ground that hinder movement and response progress. As with the case of Esther Wang, thick vegetation can obscure visual clues and impede the effectiveness of technologies like drones and helicopters, requiring SAR personnel to employ techniques that may be less efficient and effective, i.e., grid searching. GPS navigation tools and communication devices can become highly important in such environments, but GPS signals and the ability to access such environments can still be limited. Lastly, the lack of landmarks in the wilderness makes it difficult to conduct a SAR operation due to little ability to target high-hazard areas or natural environment features that may attract a missing person, thus inhibiting options to narrow down the search area and search zones.

SAR missions in water bodies (oceans, lakes, rivers) require specialized training and equipment that may be limited in policing and take longer to mobilize and deploy. And although police organizations can have diving teams/units and equipment to search for and locate people in the water (e.g., boats, divers, underwater Remote-Operated Vehicle (ROV)), finding missing persons or their remains in water has been deemed "one of the most challenging things to do because humans in water don't stay in one position and are often unreachable and hard to find" (Participant 1004). Indeed, water presents unique environmental hazards and uncontrollable conditions, namely swift currents, turbulent waters, or underwater obstructions (Byard, 2015). Visibility can be severely limited in murky or turbid waters, hampering visual SAR efforts. Adverse weather conditions, such as high winds, rough waters, or storms, can complicate inland water–related operations, impeding access or the ability to complete SAR efforts. Another challenge is that water bodies can cover considerable areas, making the operation expansive and requiring extensive resources to cover it thoroughly. The lack of defined boundaries or landmarks underwater further complicates the SAR process, making the missing person's location unknown or difficult to determine precisely. Bodies of water can conceal missing individuals, especially if they are submerged. A human body can sink, drift, or become trapped underwater because of clothing caught on rocks or plants, water depth and obstacles/structures, and decomposition gases affecting the body's buoyancy (Dennison-Wilkins, 2021). Ultimately, the complexity of these environments can make water-related SAR time-consuming and demanding, often taking longer to complete (Pearcey, 2019).

6.4.1.3 Time

SAR operations are inherently time-sensitive. Thus, "if a lot of time has elapsed, that tends to be a significant setback for SAR. We're fighting against time most of the time" (Participant 6001). For example, we spoke previously about the myth of the 24-hour rule and how delaying reporting a missing persons incident to the police can negatively affect the case. Elapsed time or time delays are "clue erasers" in SAR operations (Participant 1005). Participant 7005 explained, "We like to deploy K9 Searchers early … If time delays, then K9s are not going to be able to do a track because they pick up on the freshest human scent." Participant 14002 emphasized quick action for water-related missing persons incidents because "generally there is a 90-minute window of surviving for water-related SAR before we see it as a recovery instead of rescue." As time passes, search areas may need to be expanded, increasing the complexity and scope of the operation. SAR teams then have to cover larger territories or explore additional potential locations. This requires more resources and time to traverse every possible area thoroughly. As the operational area expands, the chances of not spotting critical clues or overlooking the missing person's location also increase.

The challenges and risks associated with going missing increase as time elapses. Factors such as exposure to the elements, fatigue, injuries, or limited access to food and water can significantly diminish a missing person's chances of survival and well-being. This is especially true in harsh environments, extreme weather conditions, or remote and inaccessible areas. Time of day is also a consideration in SAR. Participant 1006 remarked, "For example, you get a nighttime search, and you have an issue with flashlights. Well, guess what, we're going to buy a bunch of headlamps for everyone, stick it on your head, and now you go." Just as with weather and terrain, the time of the day can be connected to reduced visibility conditions and SAR equipment and personnel capabilities (e.g., harder-to-track clues at night). Various aspects related to time can thus affect the chances of locating missing individuals.

6.4.1.4 Cost and Resources

Austerity challenges have shaped policing for decades, with intense economic pressures and budget cuts at an all-time high (Brown, 2013; Huey et al., 2016). Simultaneously, police activities and the relevant tools to support this work are expanding and becoming increasingly expensive (Huey et al., 2016). This is a whole-systems challenge; both austerity policing and increasing costs and activities also impact police SAR:

> The bottom line comes down to the money. We're in a unique field where money is a factor because everybody wants to know the budget, how much everybody is getting paid, and what's all this costing. But it's unacceptable to fail somebody that's in a situation where they need help. So, it's very hard … How would you solve that? (Participant 4001)

Some SAR tools and technologies can be costly to employ. As a result, one challenge is the availability of these resources. High-end technology and specialized and advanced equipment tend to come with hefty price tags, hampering their broad availability to police organizations driven by organizational needs and demand. As Participant 13001 remarked:

> Equipment's expensive. To have what we call load-bearing vests, the Searcher's wear, we just priced them out. They're about $350 a person, so you times that by 43 people, and then you times $250 boots that are Gortex boots and times that many people, it gets expensive after a while … There's other stuff that takes precedence over a Searcher having a nice Gortex coat, so it's hard to sometimes force that agenda through the budgets when they're lean already.

This can create disparities in the capabilities and resources available to different police agencies for SAR. Yet, "the right tools for the job reduces the time needed for the SAR operation" (Participant 1002), attenuating delays in locating missing people. Managing the costs associated with the introduction and use of novel tools and technologies is imperative to ensure their augmentative, rather than detractive, impact.

Another aspect of the costs and resource challenge is the problem of allocation. Resource costs can influence decisions regarding their allocation. Limited budgets may restrict the number of police personnel deployed and the number and type of equipment assigned to a mission. At the same time, there are shortages of human resources for SAR in the policing system; participants informed that it is often the case that human resources run out long before budgets do during missions. Insufficient resources can lead to challenges in covering search areas and completing response tasks, extending the duration of the operation or compromising the effectiveness of SAR efforts. This is also connected to operational logistics challenges, such as high costs associated with transportation, fuel, accommodation, supplies, etc. To elaborate, depending on the search area's size and the operation's duration, SAR teams may need to travel long distances, establish base camps, or operate in remote locations. These logistical requirements come with financial implications for police and non-police groups. For example, one officer explained that when SAR volunteers are requested to conduct a response outside of their designated areas, "food, accommodation, and transportation costs are normally covered by the province, but this weighs in on the Incident Commanders' decision-making, all these potential costs, and they must be first approved" (Participant 6001). A potential solution for this issue is specializing police SAR to establish dedicated resources, intra- and inter-agency support, and attenuate the splitting of duties and responsibilities.

The allocation problem also relates to police not always knowing what resources can be employed. Officers explained that it can be difficult to know what resources are available for these operations because of the complex SAR system in Canada. Some discussed enhanced training on the organization of the SAR system at federal, municipal, and local levels, and time carved out while on duty to complete training, would likely be helpful, not just for SAR personnel but also for frontline patrol, bike patrol, foot patrol, and other police personnel commonly brought into SAR operations to assist. Others suggested improved oversight of these cases would be valuable to have more support for resource suggestions, with some officers explaining that they do not have Missing Persons Coordinators or Units like other agencies to provide that necessary review and assist function. Another idea was to develop resource manuals or contingency plans that are broadly accessible (e.g., via an agency's intranet) to action during these operations and offer some form of guidelines or how-tos on resources, tailored to the service's needs and considerations.

In sum, the challenges with costs and resource limitations can impact police SAR work. Dwelling on this, and explaining how these impacts span beyond just the operational environment, Participant 35002 said, "I wish there wasn't such a reliance on the cost of things. For me, it's hard to justify to a family why you're not spending the money to look for their loved one."

6.4.1.5 The Human Factor

The human factor in these missions refers to human-related challenges and complexities in the response process. SAR can be extremely demanding on personnel, with long hours, high-pressure situations, and difficult conditions. As a result, SAR teams are prone to experiencing negative sequelae themselves. Participant 3001 said:

> As a Search Manager, you got to take into account the burnout rate of your Searchers … They've been hiking for the last ten hours and we've got another six to go before we change shifts, you're just going to be ineffective at that point, right? Then it doesn't matter what your training is, you just turn into that guy like 'I just got to walk to this point that he told me to and then walk back so I can tell them I've searched it.' And not because that's what you want to do, but just your body … You can only be hyper-vigilant for so long before your body shuts closing … You have to keep that in mind.

To expand on this, officers discussed that SAR responses require sharp focus, continuous concentration, and patience to not miss clues, especially harder-to-notice signs of missing people. In operations that span several hours or days and kilometers, being so "track aware" and navigating often stressful, emergency situations can lead to fatigue and exhaustion (physical, mental, and emotional), burnout, stress, strain, anxieties, and frustration, and even fears about failing to set in. All of which can have ripple effects on the overall performance of the SAR operation. This was described as "tracker burnout or blindness" (Participant 31001). This challenge is connected to the costs and resources issue in that using the right and sufficient tools can lessen the physical, mental, and emotional demands on police during SAR responses. Further, rotating people in and out of positions, deploying a surplus of human resources, and building break times into the response can be helpful, too, as considered in the operation planning stage.

Although we explained lost persons behavior, human behavior is generally unpredictable. Thus, another human factor challenge is that missing individuals may not follow patterns or may make decisions that complicate SAR operations, such as traversing high-hazard areas or hiding from SAR personnel. Matters like panic, disorientation, age, health conditions, mental health issues, or impaired judgment and more can affect the actions and behaviors of missing persons, making it challenging to anticipate their movements or locate them. Mostly, SAR personnel are responding to unknown and unforeseeable circumstances.

An additional human factor is the involvement of multiple stakeholders, given Canada's multi-agency framework for SAR. On one side, the involvement of multiple groups brings together a range of perspectives, expertise, and experience. This diversity can enrich decision-making and contribute to comprehensive SAR strategies, resources, tools, and technologies. While collaboration among various entities is crucial for a successful operation, it can also present challenges with coordinating efforts, establishing effective communication channels, and ensuring collaboration. Indeed, these processes can be complex, particularly in large-scale operations involving multiple jurisdictions:

> If you've got several large SAR teams, if you've got SAR volunteers out there, there's radio communications, dispatch will update you, we've got the media release … Once we start compiling a large SAR, it becomes very difficult to manage all of it fast enough to do your tasks and get the next task. For the public, it's easy for them to say, 'Why didn't you do this or why can't we do this or why can't we help search?' … It takes a lot of patience and basically a lot of help at the right time … But we also … sometimes we get negative feedback from the public … like, 'Well, why didn't you do this or where did you go?' But we just need everyone's help to make this work. (Participant 1006)

Differences in training, protocols, or resources among different SAR groups can also pose coordination and information-sharing difficulties.

Moreover, human error can be a challenge. Despite often having expertise and training in SAR, police personnel can make mistakes or overlook important details during the mission. Because so many resources can get pulled into responses, especially large-scale situations including untrained officers or inexperienced citizen Searchers, it is possible that clues can be missed and errors such as search area contamination can occur. Fatigue, stress, or the pressure to find the missing person quickly can also impact personnel decision-making and hinder the effectiveness of SAR efforts. Human error can occur at any stage of the operation, from planning and organization to the actual SAR operation execution. This extends to the involvement of the public. Police SAR operations often rely on the support and cooperation of the community, from reporting sightings to providing information to participating in ground pounding. However, challenges may arise due to misinformation, false leads, or difficulties engaging the public effectively:

> Human errors, like, dealing with the family, and if the investigators are not asking the right questions or fact-checking the answers, you can get some bad information unintentionally … Media is a two-sided sword because you can sometimes get what we call 'red herrings' or bogus clues. You'll get people who have sightings of these people all over the place all of a sudden. They always say, 'Never discount a clue,' so always check it out, but don't throw all your eggs in one basket. So if somebody says they saw him walking down [street name redacted], that's great, and I'll have somebody go check, but don't stop what you're doing because you're moving everything to what could be a red herring – it might just be some guy that looks like him … You have to take all the information in, and you have to go through it and figure out what's legitimate and what's not. Where are you gonna put your resources? How are you going to allocate those things? (Participant 1004)

Weather, temperature, terrain, time, costs, resources, and the human factor are general challenges impacting SAR. We now turn to the factors that contribute to the success of police SAR work.

6.4.2 Successes

6.4.2.1 Teamwork and Collaboration

"The police can't do it all themselves … When we bring groups together, we are able to tackle whatever it is that needs to be tackled" (Participant 5003). Teamwork and collaboration are integral to the success of SAR operations to enhance resources and capabilities, share the division of labor and information, introduce skill diversity and expertise, and support these efforts. As Participant 2004 noted, "Collaboration is what's going to make the difference in doing what you do, better … We save a life doing it." Officers explained how valuable teamwork and collaboration are for receiving feedback and different perspectives and relying on others' expertise:

> It's a quick check in some circumstances, but in other circumstances, it might be something where, 'you know what, we're really stuck here, let's have a look at priors or I'm going to contact another Search Manager and liaise with them.' And I'll get that very often, where I'll have a Search Manager call me and say, "Serg, here's what we have. We've done this, we've done that', and it's like, 'OK, how about this? Have you thought about that? Have you looked at that?'. And then it's like, 'Oh no, we never really did that, or we never really thought of that.' So, a lot of times, you rely on your experiences from your peers as well. (Participant 21002)

Teamwork and collaboration are also important for sharing information between different units, groups, and personnel. In Chap. 5, it was explained that an investigation often runs concurrently with a SAR response. This intra-agency collaborative activity contributes to an operation's success, as information and leads stemming from investigative efforts inform SAR activities and vice versa. The Investigating

Officer (IO), who initially responds to a missing persons report, is vital for relaying critical details on descriptions, last known locations, and urgency determination. This information exchange can help direct SAR efforts and establish case priority and resource allocation. Many other examples of intra-agency collaboration related to information sharing are detailed throughout this book, from Emergency Call-Takers and Dispatchers (ECDs) to Missing Persons Units to LE Analysts.

Since Canada's SAR system involves a range of local and national bodies, public service agents, and groups and organizations, intra- and inter-group teamwork and collaboration allow for resource allocation and optimization. Agencies and groups can share equipment, personnel, and logistical support. This can prevent resource shortages, enhance operational capacity, and increase the overall efficiency of the operation. This can also attenuate some of the issues with the high costs associated with SAR resources:

> Say we have a person who is despondent, they've gone missing, and they're near waterways, and we have information they may be there. We'll call the fire department right away because we wanted to search that area, and they'll grab their search crew, their search team, and that doesn't cost us any money because that comes out of their budget … Is there a cost to all this? There sure is if you have to call police resources in. But other groups like volunteers and firefighters reduce our costs and are a huge, huge help … We utilize their resources, they utilize ours, and we'll work together in getting through the case … If we need them, they're out. Volunteers are a great resource, a great bunch of people to utilize, they come out, they do their thing, they help us in every regard. (Participant 11005)

While these factors impact the success of SAR operations, collaboration across the many partners and groups can be weak. For instance, as police and non-police groups across Canada have their own protocols and procedures, interoperability challenges emerge that impact teamwork and collaboration. We explain some solutions to this in Chap. 7—there remain opportunities to improve teamwork and collaboration.

6.4.2.2 Frontloading Resources and Resource Allocation

Frontloading resources refers to the practice of allocating a significant portion of resources at the early stages of a SAR response. Participant 1002 explained, "If you frontload all of the resources that you can, that greatly, greatly increases your chance of success because it first allows for rapid and immediate response." It ensures that personnel, equipment, and support are readily available and have been mobilized into action. This ultimately can contribute to improved operational efficiency by eliminating delays if efforts need to be scaled up. It can be quicker and easier to scale down and is of benefit to the missing person if a surplus of personnel and equipment are available for the operation versus requesting additional resources amid a response and waiting for these to mobilize and deploy. This relates to effective resource utilization in that anticipating the potential demands of a situation and allocating resources accordingly helps police avoid the last-minute scramble for personnel or equipment. Frontloading can increase SAR capacity from the start, as it means more hands and tools are available to complete activities. But, this is not sufficient alone; police also have to deploy the right resources and do so at the appropriate times:

> Putting the resources in at the right time … If you have a situation where you have what we categorize as a Level 1 'Emergency' search, that's where we have to have a Search Manager initiated. We have to have an Incident Commander involved. We have to have search-trained personnel, which could include the K9 Unit … If we have the right situation, we can throw the K9 Unit out there, and we can get some success with that in locating the person that's missing. (Participant 12002)

Using the "right" resources refers to employing the most appropriate tools, technology, and personnel suited to the needs and requirements of a particular SAR task or situation and aligned with the operation's objectives. Different responses will require different tools and expertise depending on factors like environment, weather conditions, terrain, or characteristics of the missing person. Determining what is "right" can stem from the agency's "best practices," past operations, case studies and lessons learned, known SAR techniques such as lost persons behavior and search theory, and the expertise of SAR personnel. The "right" resources also means police SAR personnel need to be trained and prepared for these missions to add the necessary expertise. Police explained that various training and professional development activities can contribute to the success of SAR operations with the "right" resources, including mock field-based scenarios, in-house refresher courses, workshops, presentations, completing Search Management courses, and harnessing case studies and lessons learned. However, as highlighted in a paper on training police SAR teams in Canada using a dataset of the interview and survey data employed in this book, "training police personnel in SAR operations is haphazard at best, contingent on the agency prioritizing SAR work and often absent provincial or federal mandate or guidance. This lack of homogeneous, structured, and/or standardized training offerings for police SAR personnel creates inefficiencies that can have enormous implications for the successful location of missing persons" (Ferguson & Gaub, 2021, p. 446). Hence, improved police training for the provision of the right resources is likely to have positive impacts on these operations and the field more broadly.[1]

6.4.2.3 Communication

"Communication is key not just in missing persons, but in all aspects of policing," Participant 1005 stated. Good communication facilitates effective coordination, information sharing, and decision-making among parties involved in SAR. "Good communication" was broadly conceptualized as clear, concise, timely, responsive, steadfast, reliable, two-way, collaborative, and informative. Clear and concise

[1] See Ferguson and Gaub (2023) for some training needs and recommendations that explain what could be improved.

communication ensures that everyone understands the information being shared, minimizing the risk of misinterpretation or confusion. Conciseness can be particularly valuable to not take up unnecessary time to understand and further relay messages, especially because of the time-sensitive nature of these operations. Being timely and responsive means that communications are conveyed promptly and reach the relevant parties rapidly. Quick response times to incoming messages or requests attenuate delays in information-sharing that might hinder SAR efforts, decision-making, and the overall efficiency of the operation.

Furthermore, standardized communication procedures were emphasized as crucial in each SAR operation. Having established communication protocols ensures consistency and clarity in message delivery. Standardized codes, terminology, and formats help prevent misunderstandings and facilitate efficient communication. Establishing active two-way communication options and the voice, hand, and other signal communications that will be utilized in the response during the planning stage, and importantly communicated to all SAR personnel during the mobilization and operational phase can be vital. Two-way communication includes not only relaying information from the command post to SAR teams in the field but also encouraging teams to provide updates, observations, and requests for support for ensuring information flows and all parties are engaged and properly resourced. Communication signals can include radio operations, whistle calls that will be used when a clue is found and ways in which to communicate with the command post during ground pounding, among other important instructions.

Communication technology can lose battery, cut out, lose signal, and be interfered with depending upon the weather and terrain. For example, Participant 5004 discussed that during an operation in a rugged, remote area that involved SAR teams being split by a mountain range, "reliable communication was severely limited, and we regularly lost communications with each other due to terrain interference. To this day, I still feel like we could have found them quicker if we could've had reliable communication." For these reasons, having multiple methods and backup plans for communications contribute to the success of SAR operations. Good communication ensures access to several channels to reach all relevant parties and builds in redundant options. This may include radio communication, digital platforms, phone calls, or in-person check-ins. It can also allow for flexibility, enabling different SAR teams or agencies to use the communication method that works best for them. These altogether embody what is considered "good communication" in police SAR work.

References

Bennett, K., & Ferguson, L. (2022). Police responses to cold and long-term missing person cases: A comparative study. International Journal of Comparative and Applied Criminal Justice, 1–21. https://doi.org/10.1080/01924036.2022.2094433

Brimicombe, A. (2016). Analysing police-recorded data 1. *Legal Information Management, 16*(2), 71–77.

Brodeur, J. P., & Dupont, B. (2006). Knowledge workers or "knowledge" workers? *Policing and Society, 16*(1), 7–26.
Brown, J. M. (Ed.). (2013). *The future of policing*. Routledge.
Byard, R. W. (2015). Immersion deaths and drowning: Issues arising in the investigation of bodies recovered from water. *Forensic Science, Medicine, and Pathology, 11*, 323–325.
Canadian Press. (2023). *Rescuers praise teen hiker Esther Wang, found safe after two days lost in B.C. park*. Retrieved from https://www.thecanadianpressnews.ca/environment/rescuers-praise-teen-hiker-esther-wang-found-safe-after-two-days-lost-in-b-c/article_f84e046e-bb9d-571b-8d96-3338ee3d6646.html
Dennison-Wilkins, L. (2021). *Body recovery from water study*. College of Policing. Retrieved from https://www.college.police.uk/article/body-recovery-water-study
Ericson, R. (1982). *Reproducing order: A study of police patrol work*. Toronto Press.
Ferguson, L. (2022). "Giving the highest chance of a good outcome": Exploring the missing persons act in British Columbia and Ontario from the policing perspective. *Canadian Journal of Criminology and Criminal Justice, 64*(4), 69–87.
Ferguson, L., & Gaub, J. E. (2021). Training police search and rescue teams: Implications for missing persons work. *Criminology & Criminal Justice*. https://doi.org/10.1177/17488958211057380
Ferguson, L., & Sidebottom, A. (2022). Policing and missing persons. In *Oxford research encyclopedia of criminology and criminal justice*. Retrieved from https://oxfordre.com/criminology/display/10.1093/acrefore/9780190264079.001.0001/acrefore-9780190264079-e-725
Ferguson, L., & Gaub, J. E. (2023). Training police search and rescue teams: Implications for missing persons work. *Criminology & Criminal Justice, 23*(3), 431–449.
Giacomantonio, C. (2015). *Policing integration: The sociology of police coordination work*. Palgrave Macmillan.
Gouda, K. (2023). Teen hiker Esther Wang speaks out after being lost in the woods for over two days. *Global News*. Retrieved from: https://globalnews.ca/news/9808001/teen-hiker-esther-wang-speaks-out-after-being-stuck-in-the-woods-for-over-two-days/
Huey, L., Cyr, K., & Ricciardelli, R. (2016). Austerity policing's imperative: Understanding the drivers of policing activity in Canada. *International Journal of Police Science & Management, 18*(2), 133–139.
Huey, L., Ricciardelli, R., & Ferguson, L. (2022a). "You don't need 55 forms that say the same thing": The Burden on police to produce extra-institutional knowledge. *Crime & Delinquency*. https://doi.org/10.1177/00111287221134045
Huey, L., Ferguson, L., & Koziarski, J. (2022b). The irrationalities of rationality in police data processes. *Policing and Society, 32*(8), 947–962.
Luen, T. W., & Al-Hawamdeh, S. (2001). Knowledge management in the public sector: Principles and practices in police work. *Journal of Information Science, 27*(5), 311–318.
Malm, A., Pollard, N., Brantingham, P., et al. (2005). *A 30 year analysis of police service delivery and costing: 'E' division*. Retrieved from https://www.ufv.ca/media/assets/ccjr/ccjr-resources/ccjr-publications/30_Year_Analysis__%28English%29.pdf
McSheffrey, E. (2023). 16-year-old girl separated from group, missing after hike in B.C.'s Golden Ears Park. *Global News*. Retrieved from https://globalnews.ca/news/9799401/16-year-old-girl-missing-golden-ears-park-bc/
Pearcey, J. (2019). *Water-related missing persons operations*. Retrieved from https://www.fireengineering.com/technical-rescue/water-related-missing-persons/#gref
Reilly, P. (2023). Lost 16-year-old hiker walks out of Canadian wilderness on her own after frantic 54-hour search. *New York Post*. Retrieved from https://nypost.com/2023/07/02/esther-wang-16-walks-out-of-canadian-wilderness-after-frantic-search/
Shalev, K., Schaefer, M., & Morgan, A. (2009). Investigating missing person cases: How can we learn where they go or how far they travel? *International Journal of Police Science & Management, 11*(2), 123–129.

Chapter 7
Outroduction to Police Search and Rescue

7.1 Improvements to Police Search and Rescue

Advancements in tools and technologies and collaboration have improved police search and rescue (SAR) work. "When I started doing SAR 25 years ago to today, the difference is incredible. The way we do things now is much better" (Participant 1005). Some of the stories introducing each chapter have been a part of these developments. Chap. 1 starts with Burton Winters, who tragically froze to death on sea ice following a snowmobile accident. Some seven years after his death, an inquiry into SAR in Newfoundland and Labrador was spurred by Burton's family's pleas for answers for what they described as an "indifferent response" from SAR agencies. This identified 17 recommendations to improve SAR in the province, including police enacting policies to ensure follow-up with families of the missing that involve the provision of trauma-informed counseling, and mental health training for police SAR personnel (Igloliorte, 2021). A Labrador journalist later chronicled Burton's story to reflect on the concerted public effort "to wrest something positive out of the terrible tragedy" (SaltWire Network, 2017).

We also told the story of Daniel Trask, whose remains were discovered after three and a half years by MibSAR volunteers in the wilderness of northern Ontario (MibSAR, 2013). Maureen Trask, his mother, has been a trailblazer in the field, propelled by the challenges and struggles she endured in the course to locate Daniel. Among many tasks, she advocated for Ontario legislation, the *Missing Persons Act* enacted in 2019, to improve police powers to respond to missing persons because her experiences navigating the process were "unbearable, inconsistent, and unfair" (Trask, 2021). In speaking with journalists, Maureen explained that the roadblocks families and police face in the response to missing persons were "shocking" and that when asking the police, "Well could [Daniel] be in a hospital? Could he have had an accident when he first went missing?" They said, "Well you would have to

L. Ferguson, L. Huey, *Police Search and Rescue Response to Lost and Missing Persons*, SpringerBriefs in Criminology,
https://doi.org/10.1007/978-3-031-44077-9_7

check with local hospitals because we don't have authority" (CBC News, 2019). It is an Act inspired by a mother.

These stories are not the only incidents that have had ripple effects. For example, the truths of more than 2,380 people in the National Inquiry into Missing and Murdered Indigenous Women (MMIWG) (2019) led to 231 Calls for Justice to change this field. Or, around seven years earlier, the stories of the over 20 women who went missing and were murdered by serial killer Robert Pickton in British Columbia—and the failures of police in these investigations—led to the Missing Women Commission of Inquiry (Oppal, 2012). This outlined 63 recommendations, including innovation and standardization in police responses to missing persons (Oppal, 2012). There are many, many others. Throughout these pages, we took up a task publicly called for uncovering the police response to these cases, focusing specifically on SAR work. While there have been improvements, there is still much to be done, and it will always be the case that societal changes will demand adjustments to policing and SAR. Therefore, we conclude this book by addressing the question "What may be next?" in the police SAR response to missing persons in Canada.

7.2 Future Trends

We have discussed that the work police are expected to complete is expanding, involving more complicated situations, human problems, and tasks. At the same time, police face austerity challenges such as budget constraints, reduced resources, and often limited organizational and operational support for SAR. In a landscape like this, what does the future of this work look like? Though we cannot anticipate everything that will happen over the next several years, this section is mindful of the emerging trends likely to impact both the demand for police SAR in Canada and how police respond to missing persons.

7.2.1 Climate Change

Moving into future years, changing climatic conditions will likely become highly relevant to these operations. Temperatures over land have been rising, extreme weather events have increased, the duration of ice cover in the reaches of Northern Canada (and globally) is decreasing, and water levels are rising (Ford et al., 2015; Clark et al., 2016), all of which are relevant to SAR. While the exact implications of climate change on this area of police work are uncertain, it is anticipated that the capacity of SAR teams and the number of operations may be affected. This is already happening. For instance, in Nunavut, Canada, Chadburn et al. (2017) found that thinner and more dangerous ice conditions have increased the amount of SAR missions. Clark et al. (2016) also found an increased risk for personnel when conducting SAR in Nunavut due to the effects of climate change, such as more incidents of SAR members falling through the ice. Chap. 6 noted how climate impacts SAR operations (e.g., resource efficiency and effectiveness) and the risk to people while missing. These challenges may be heightened in future years. Thus, there may be a greater emphasis on resilience, preparedness, and adaptation for police. Possible future topical areas related to climate change include the following: How do the police adapt? What additional training is required for police SAR to navigate climate impacts? What SAR equipment and supplies must be retained, developed, or upgraded?

7.2.2 Aging Population of Canada

The twenty-first century has been marked by an era of global population aging, constituting a new phenomenon in human history. People are living longer, and there is a shift in the population age structure toward older ages (World Health Organization, 2022). Policymakers face challenges with the economic impacts (e.g., fewer working-age people) and implementing sustainable policy and funding solutions for care and servicing (e.g., greater demands for health and retirement programs). This, too, is likely to shape the future path of policing, SAR, and missing persons. As the population ages, increased incidents of older adults going missing will likely occur due to the positive relationship between age, cognitive decline, and missing persons (Kowalski, 2020; Neubauer et al., 2021). This group also often experiences physical and other limitations such as reduced mobility, vision or hearing impairments, and chronic medical conditions. When elderly individuals go missing, these factors can make it more challenging to navigate their environments or (re)orient themselves. Furthermore, these factors heighten vulnerability and risk levels when missing, so there may be more urgency during SAR missions and emergencies requiring police response, thereby leading to an increased demand for police SAR. Police may need to address the unique needs of the aging population—for instance, training on common age-related ailments and techniques for communicating with and assisting older individuals. Police SAR may also need to adapt their SAR strategies, including collaborating with community organizations and healthcare providers to develop comprehensive response plans tailored to the needs of older adults. The impact of an aging population on police SAR and missing persons needs tracking, assessment, and strategies.

7.2.3 Technology

Guidelines and legislation on new technologies are forming to add boundaries on their use, criteria for who can operate them, and certification requirements. Chap. 3 discussed wearable technology for vulnerable persons. An emerging conversation is the ethical and human rights considerations of their function. Questions arise regarding vulnerable people's ability to consent to their use, the restriction to a person's liberty, and their invasion of privacy (Etis, 2005; Wangmo et al., 2019). As these conversations advance, what may be the impact on police practice and policy and their use and utility in locating missing persons? Furthermore, as the Government of Canada (2013) explains, "New technologies have the potential to create a false sense of security amongst the general public. For instance, with a GPS in hand, Canadians may be more willing to trek into increasingly remote areas, thereby increasing the potential for a SAR incident" (p. 15). What can be done to attenuate SAR technology–related challenges and concerns? How can technologies be best used for locating missing persons? Such questions will be highly relevant as technological changes continue. It will be crucial to strike a balance between embracing technological advancements and maintaining the importance of human judgment, experience, ethics, and supporting regulation in police SAR moving forward.

Police may leverage technologies beyond operational settings. Virtual and augmented reality offer potential training, planning, and situational awareness applications. Simulations can provide realistic training environments to practice SAR scenarios, while augmented reality could overlay critical information, such as maps, onto a search area for enhanced situational awareness (Shi et al., 2021; LaLone et al., 2019; Hu et al., 2022). Virtual and augmented reality can replicate challenging SAR situations (e.g., water), enabling personnel to gain valuable experience in a mock, controlled setting. Also, artificial intelligence and machine learning algorithms can process large volumes of data for SAR missions, including social media feeds, surveillance footage, and historical records, to identify patterns and potential leads in missing persons cases, among other applications (Laperrière-Robillard et al., 2022; Mengash et al., 2023). These hypotheticals are additional technological innovations that may become useful in this work with time.

One limitation with new technologies is that there needs to be the infrastructure within policing—i.e., people available and capable of using it, training on their applications—for their utility in SAR. Having the advanced technology available to police is not sufficient alone, as there must be the resources designated to become proficient at using it. In addition, timely and consistent technology adoption may continue to prove difficult. Implementing and maintaining advanced SAR technologies can be costly, especially for smaller police organizations with limited budgets and resources. These constraints can result in non-uniform technology standards or disparities in technological capabilities among different SAR entities. Unequal access to technology across the policing system, and with non-police groups, can impede interoperability and collaboration. Interoperability challenges may spawn from different or incompatible police services adopting systems, software, and equipment. Addressing ethical and guideline or legal considerations, integrating technologies, and ensuring utility and interoperability will help harness the potential of new technologies and maximize their positive impact in SAR.

7.2.4 Collaboration

Future years will involve continuing to strengthen collaborative partnerships and interoperability to share resources, expertise, and information, enhancing a coordinated and efficient response to missing persons incidents. "It just comes down to time and just getting it together to collaborate," Participant 1002 explained, "As I say, the more collaboration you have with people that are doing what you do will make you better at what you're doing. Makes you think more outside of the box."

Officers discussed shared databases and communication platforms, and balancing standardization with case-by-case responses, to enable seamless coordination and information exchange between police and non-police groups and across policing. Participant 3003 said, "It'd be good to have one repository for all of police SAR data, and then some portal to share information and insights back and forth with our SAR volunteers like case studies and whatnot." Participant 1004 proposed "some sort of national program that combined us all together to share information … That would be incredible." The future of SAR may involve exploring opportunities for standardization (e.g., in data collection/sharing and response procedures)—while remaining mindful of the benefit of the Canadian SAR system deriving from diverse and tailored approaches. Forming local, regional, and national networks was noted for collaboration and facilitating information sharing between SAR groups. Suggestions included task forces, working groups, centralized centers or hubs, and conferences in and for Canada. These were also thought useful for police to develop an improved awareness of the external SAR resources in their region and Canada to know when and how to engage such groups in these operations and improve their utility. For interoperability, joint training and establishing coordinated command structures are directions officers see the field moving toward to enhance SAR capabilities and foster effective response in multi-agency operations. Standardized or integrated training programs and protocols could improve interoperability by ensuring all police and non-police SAR personnel receive consistent instruction on the relevant roles and responsibilities, and do so jointly to establish a clear understanding of mandates, boundaries, and what the role of each group is during these missions.

There is also profound recognition of the need for improved collaboration between the police and families and loved ones of the missing. In this instance, when we say "collaboration," we mean improved police engagement and communication with families and loved ones during and after response efforts. The several inquiries and reviews spanning multiple decades into police search and investigative failures and faults related to missing persons reveal a persistent narrative that much more work needs to be done in this area. In 2006, Pfeifer, in writing about missing persons police practice and policy, documented "frustration with issues related to communication between families and the police" (p. 8). Fifteen years later, the Office of the Federal Ombudspersons for Victims of Crime (2021) remarked, "Families with a missing loved one have voiced that the primary reason for their dissatisfaction with police services is the lack of timely action, sensitivity, and communication. A lack of timely information has been noted as most concerning for families of missing persons." These are just two examples highlighting persistent collaboration issues between the police and families and loved ones of the missing in Canada, but there are more (see Oppal, 2012; Pearce, 2013; Humans Rights Watch, 2013; MMIWG, 2019).

What can be done to improve this problem in future years? Multiple suggestions have been offered by families and loved ones, in inquiries and reviews, and from the policing perspective. Epstein (2021) recommended that police develop a communication plan with affected families and loved ones and look to establish an in-agency Family Liaison Team during incidents and cold/long-term cases. Pfeifer (2006) suggested that police expand the role of Victim Services to include responding to the needs of families and loved ones, as well as missing persons, throughout incidents, filling this gap on the policing side. Trask (2020) provided suggestions from the families' perspective, including (1) communication on the resources available for SAR, (2) explaining SAR decisions and engaging in collaboration on such processes (e.g., explaining why a mission is or is not being conducted), and (3) coordinating SAR logistics and execution with families. Collaboration with families and loved ones is an important area moving forward in the field, given the seemingly interminable nature of this issue yet years of proposals to improve the situation.

7.2.5 Data

There is a push in policing to collect, analyze, and store data from incidents and complete various knowledge work activities such as paperwork for reasons such as "cover your ass" culture, fulfilling extra-institutional requirements, evidence-based policing, and for proactive, analytical police work (Ericson, 1982; Ericson & Haggerty, 1997; Malm et al., 2005; Huey et al., 2022). When writing this book, there is no national, centralized, or standardized accounting of police SAR activities. Information on the rate of SAR incidents, their nature, and the effectiveness of this police response varies widely from jurisdiction to jurisdiction and agency to agency. Accurate and comparable data on police SAR in Canada is needed, such as to provide valuable insights into police SAR effectiveness and efficiency. First, data-driven decision-making is becoming increasingly important in policing. During operations, leveraging data can help police SAR determine the most effective search patterns, deployment strategies, and resource allocation, leading to more efficient and targeted operations. For post-operations, centralized and standardized data would allow police to evaluate their response times, success rates, resource allocation, and other key performance indicators. This information can assist in identifying areas for improvement, optimizing strategies, and enhancing overall operational effectiveness. This said, there needs to be the infrastructure to collect, store, clean, manage, and analyze data for these benefits to come to fruition (see note on the use of Law Enforcement (LE) Analysts below). Another need is publicly available data to foster independent study into what works, what does not, and what needs improvement.

7.2.6 A Focus on Prevention

Prevention often falls secondary to response efforts in policing for many reasons. For example, resource limitations hinder police allocation to prevention efforts. Individuals at risk of going missing, particularly vulnerable populations, may be hesitant to engage with police due to stigma or fear of legal consequences, creating barriers to reaching and providing support to those in need. However, policymaker inaction (e.g., no funding solutions) and social and health services "downloading" problems onto the police are consistent prevention inhibitors (Huey et al., 2022). Missing persons is an example of this reality. Years of international research have shown that some primary drivers of police missing persons service calls are social and health services such as hospitals and care homes (Bartholomew et al., 2009; Sowerby & Thomas, 2017; Ferguson & Huey, 2020). To cope with their own institutional limits, these services dump responsibility to the police for locating and returning clients, all while the duty of care and safeguarding rests with them (Huey et al., 2022). Preventing missing persons extends beyond the police's scope or abilities to bar the trickle-down effect of other groups transferring their response and prevention duties. A chunk of the work required for preventing missing persons and, thus, SAR incidents is actually beyond the sole ability of police, instead requiring multi-agency collaboration, government solutions, and a willingness by policymakers to make considerable efforts to tackle this thorny social issue (e.g., work across institutions, invest in long-term strategies and sustained commitment).

That said, a focus on prevention in policing is needed. Layering the potential rise in missing persons reports requiring SAR with the possible increase in challenges and complexities associated with these events, and the austerity challenges police face, all point to the necessity of prevention efforts. Preventing incidents is generally more cost-effective than responding to emergencies, avoiding the need for deploying expensive resources and conducting large-scale operations, thus reducing strains across the policing system. This is not to say that these efforts do not broadly happen. On the day-to-day, police are engaged in enforcement and regulation activities, such as ensuring compliance with boating regulations and hiking permits to prevent water- and wilderness-related SAR incidents. However, as noted, there is a long history in policing of not placing enough emphasis on prevention (Oppal, 2012; Epstein, 2020).

A focus on prevention is integrating activities into the work of police that avert incidents before they occur. A number of suggestions were made by officers for this—the primary relating to funding and resources. As touched on above, one is improving the capacity and capability of health and social services to safeguard and manage their clients, along with managing missing persons incidents. Other suggestions were funding and resources for targeting high-risk groups. Participant 1009 gave the example, "A fully funded program for persons at risk of wandering should be implemented once a diagnosis is made for those individuals by a specialist. It should be an automatic process that requires no effort by family members." Officers extended the need for funded intervention programs for persons who go repeatedly missing too. Increased funding and resources in the policing system for SAR were suggested so as to have the right and enough personnel and tools to engage in these efforts, such as specializing this work, as noted in Chap. 2. This was linked to the need for enough and appropriate[1] resources to engage in proactive policing strategies, including conducting welfare checks on vulnerable individuals; establishing regular communication means with at-risk populations; building strong partnerships with community organizations, social service agencies, mental health professionals, and other stakeholders to better identify individuals at risk, provide early interventions, and connect individuals with appropriate support services; and developing and delivering educational programs and awareness campaigns to the community (e.g., on outdoor safety, navigation skills, and the importance of informing others about travel plans). All require funding and resources, which many police services across Canada do not have specifically for missing persons and SAR.

Another proposal was leveraging existing resources, such as improved use of LE Analysts in this work for proactivity and being data driven. For prevention efforts, officers suggested LE Analysts be used to analyze case and operational data to, for example, identify commonalities and trends that can inform prevention strategies targeted toward high-risk populations or areas, develop data-driven risk assessment models or tools, and engage in geographic profiling to find spatial patterns in cases to pinpoint high-risk zones or hotspots for targeting with community engagement. More and better training, and dedicated on-duty time to complete it, for police on SAR was suggested for prevention efforts too. For instance, specialized training on identifying signs of vulnerability, mental health issues, substance abuse, or other factors that may contribute to someone going missing were mentioned for the provision of appropriate and adequate support and services, which can potentially prevent incidents from occurring.

7.2.7 Research and Evidence-Based SAR

A movement toward evidence-based SAR (EBSAR) may be upon us as a part of the global drive toward evidence-based policing, which aims to create and use the best available research evidence to inform and guide police practice and policy (Sherman, 1998; Piza & Welsh, 2021). However, the landscape of Canadian police SAR research is barren. A combination of no publicly available data, lack of attention on or recognition of this work, and a focus on internally produced lessons learned and case studies collected from operations to inform policy and practice means that there is not much capacity to conduct and implement research in this space. The absence of data alone generally inhibits the ability of researchers to study police

[1] "Appropriate" means engaged officers with experience and expertise in missing person investigations and SAR.

SAR. These issues are interdependent, too; a reliance on internal case studies by police SAR likely stems from the lack of research to employ.

Without a solid research foundation, it becomes challenging to identify effective strategies, optimal resources, and appropriate training methods in SAR. Limited research can also restrict the understanding of emerging trends, evolving challenges, and best practices, making it difficult to stay updated on advancements in the field—such as with technology, search theory, risk assessment, and incident management—that could enhance the effectiveness and efficiency of this work. This can affect the credibility and recognition of SAR as a distinct field of study and practice. The minimal research might hinder securing the necessary funding, support, and resources for prevention initiatives, equipment upgrades, and professional development opportunities for SAR personnel. The implications of limited research and scholarly attention on police SAR are plenty.

EBSAR would involve police utilizing research to inform and guide SAR decision-making and operations. It would first require systematically collecting and analyzing data, conducting research in collaboration (police, non-police, academics), evaluating existing studies, and incorporating the best available research into SAR policies, protocols, and training. In the future, EBSAR will probably be driven by progressions in technology, increased data demands, and the growing recognition of the importance of research in optimizing police work. For example, evidence-based approaches can help evaluate the effectiveness and practicality of emerging technologies such as Unmanned Aerial Vehicles (UAVs) and Artificial intelligence (AI). An EBSAR movement would foster collaboration among SAR agencies and groups, and research institutions—a much-needed enterprise. By sharing data, best practices, and research findings, the SAR community can build a comprehensive evidence base, leading to more informed decision-making and improved SAR and missing persons outcomes.

References

Bartholomew, D., Duffy, D., & Figgins, N. (2009). *Strategies to reduce missing patients. A practical workbook. National Mental Health Development Unit*. Retrieved from http://www.nmhdu.org.uk/silo/files/a-strategy-to-reduce-missing-patients--a-practicalworkbook.pdf

CBC News. (2019). *New missing persons act gives Ontario police more power to investigate*. Retrieved from https://www.cbc.ca/news/canada/kitchener-waterloo/ontario-missing-persons-act-maureen-trask-1.5164532#:~:text=CBC%20News%20Loaded-,New%20Missing%20Persons%20act%20gives%20Ontario%20police%20more%20power%20to,son%20Daniel%20disappeared%20in%202011

Chadburn, S. E., Burke, E. J., Cox, P. M., Friedlingstein, P., Hugelius, G., & Westermann, S. (2017). An observation-based constraint on permafrost loss as a function of global warming. *Nature Climate Change, 7*(5), 340–344.

Clark, D. G., Ford, J. D., Pearce, T., & Berrang-Ford, L. (2016). Vulnerability to unintentional injuries associated with land-use activities and search and rescue in Nunavut, Canada. *Social Science & Medicine, 169*, 18–26.

Etis, K. (2005). *Society's most vulnerable under surveillance: The ethics of tagging and tracking dementia patients with GPS technology: A comparative view*. Oxford U Comparative L Forum. Retrieved from https://ouclf.law.ox.ac.uk/societys-most-vulnerable-under-surveillance-the-ethics-of-tagging-and-tracking-dementia-patients-with-gps-technology-a-comparative-view/

Ericson, R. V. (1982). *Reproducing order: A study of police patrol work*. Toronto, ON: University of Toronto Press.

Ericson, R. V., & Haggerty, K. D. (1997). *Policing the risk society*. Toronto, ON: University of Toronto Press. Malm.

Epstein, G. (2020). *Missing and Missed - Report of The Independent Civilian Review into Missing Person Investigations*. Retrieved from https://www.tps.ca/chief/chiefs-office/missing-and-missed-implementation/report-independent-civilian-review-missing-person-investigations/

Epstein, J. (2021). *Missing and missed: Report of the independent civilian review into missing persons investigations*. Retrieved from https://8e5a70b5-92aa-40ae-a0bd-e885453ee64c.filesusr.com/ugd/a94b60_65605a078ad543ca936f8daa67ea4772.pdf?index=true

Ferguson, L., & Huey, L. (2020). Who is reported missing from Canadian hospitals and mental health units? *Policing: An International Journal, 43*(3), 525–540.

Ford, J. D., McDowell, G., & Pearce, T. (2015). The adaptation challenge in the Arctic. *Nature Climate Change, 5*(12), 1046–1053.

Government of Canada. (2013). *Quadrennial search and rescue review*. Retrieved from https://www.publicsafety.gc.ca/cnt/rsrcs/pblctns/archive-nss-qdrnnl-rvw/archive-nss-qdrnnl-rvw-en.pdf

Hu, D., Chen, L., Du, J., Cai, J., & Li, S. (2022). Seeing through disaster rubble in 3D with ground-penetrating radar and interactive augmented reality for urban search and rescue. *Journal of Computing in Civil Engineering, 36*(5), 04022021.

Huey, L., Ferguson, L., & Koziarski, J. (2022). The irrationalities of rationality in police data processes. *Policing and Society, 32*(8), 947–962.

Humans Rights Watch. (2013). *Those who take us away: Abusive policing and failures in protection of indigenous women and girls in Northern British Columbia, Canada*. Retrieved from https://www.hrw.org/report/2013/02/13/those-who-take-us-away/abusive-policing-and-failures-protection-indigenous-women

Igloliorte, J. (2021). *Public inquiry respecting ground search and rescue for lost and missing persons*. Retrieved from https://www.nlgsarinquiry.ca/final-report/

Kowalski, L. (2020). *Hiding in plain sight: A mixed methods analysis of older adults who are reported missing in two Canadian cities*. Retrieved from https://search.proquest.com/openview/1c3a99464fb55bd766ea39ba8fd0940e/1?pq-origsite=gscholar&cbl=18750&diss=y

LaLone, N., Alharthi, S. A., & Toups, Z. O. (2019). A vision of augmented reality for urban search and rescue. In *Proceedings of the halfway to the future symposium* (pp. 1–4).

Laperrière-Robillard, T., Morin, M., & Abi-Zeid, I. (2022). Supervised learning for maritime search operations: An artificial intelligence approach to search efficiency evaluation. *Expert Systems with Applications, 206*, 117857.

Malm, A., Pollard, N., Brantingham, P., Tinsley, P., Plecas, D., Brantingham, P., ... & Kinney, B. (2005). *A 30 year analysis of police service delivery and costing: "E" division*. Retrieved from https://www.publicsafety.gc.ca/lbrr/archives/cnmcs-plcng/cn000042150791-eng.pdf

Mengash, H. A., Alzahrani, J. S., Eltahir, M. M., Al-Wesabi, F. N., Mohamed, A., Hamza, M. A., & Marzouk, R. (2023). Search and rescue optimization with machine learning enabled cyber-security model. *Computer Systems Science & Engineering, 45*(2).

Michigan Backcountry Search and Rescue (MibSAR). (2013). *Daniel Trask's home page*. Retrieved from http://www.mibsar.com/Cases/Trask/Trask.html [May 27, 2023].

MMIWG. (2019). *Reclaiming power and place: The final report of the national inquiry into missing and murdered indigenous women and girls*. Retrieved from https://www.mmiwg-ffada.ca/final-report/

Neubauer, N. A., Miguel-Cruz, A., & Liu, L. (2021). *Strategies to locate lost persons with dementia: a case study of Ontario first responders*. Retrieved from https://www.hindawi.com/journals/jar/2021/5572764/

Oppal, W. (2012). *Forsaken: The report of the missing women commission of inquiry*. Retrieved from https://missingwomen.library.uvic.ca/index.html

Pearce, M. (2013). *An awkward silence: Missing and murdered vulnerable women and the Canadian justice system*. Retrieved from https://ruor.uottawa.ca/handle/10393/26299

Pfeifer, J. (2006). *Missing persons in Saskatchewan: Police policy and practice*. Retrieved from https://pubsaskdev.blob.core.windows.net/pubsask-prod/86185/86185-Jeff_Pfeifer_Report_on_Missing_Persons_-_Police_Policy_and_Practice.pdf

Piza, E. L., & Welsh, B. C. (Eds.). (2021). *The globalization of evidence-based policing: Innovations in bridging the research-practice divide*. New York: Routledge.

SaltWire Network. (2017). *Burton winters: The Labrador boy who walked into history*. Retrieved from https://www.saltwire.com/newfoundland-labrador/holidays/burton-winters-the-labrador-boy-who-walked-into-history-28316/ [May 28, 2023].

Sherman, L. (1998). *Evidence-based policing* (Ideas in American policing lecture series). Police Foundation.

Shi, Y., Kang, J., Xia, P., Tyagi, O., Mehta, R. K., & Du, J. (2021). Spatial knowledge and firefighters' wayfinding performance: A virtual reality search and rescue experiment. *Safety Science, 139*, 105231.

Sowerby, A., & Thomas, S. D. (2017). A mixed methods study of the mental health and criminal justice histories of missing persons. *Police Practice and Research, 18*(1), 87–98.

Trask, M. (2020). Missing persons – Recommendations. https://www.academia.edu/41995080/Missing_Persons_Recommendations.

Trask, M. (2021). *Missing persons from the families perspective*. Retrieved from https://www.missingpersonsresearchhub.com/post/missing-persons-from-the-families-perspective

Wangmo, T., Lipps, M., Kressig, R. W., & Ienca, M. (2019). Ethical concerns with the use of intelligent assistive technology: Findings from a qualitative study with professional stakeholders. *BMC Medical Ethics, 20*(1), 1–11.

World Health Organization. (2022). *Ageing and health*. Retrieved from https://www.who.int/news-room/fact-sheets/detail/ageing-and-health

Appendix: The Data

As noted in Chap. 1, this book presents findings from an analysis of various data related to police involvement with lost and missing persons in Canada. The below table depicts the details of these data (see Table A.1).

These data were pooled and then coded thematically according to one of our six chapter themes: background and information on search and rescue in Canada; the organization of police search and rescue; the launch of police search and rescue; the work of police search and rescue (two chapters, one theme); the events after police search and rescue response; and the outroduction on police search and rescue in Canada. We then synthesized our thematic findings to create datasets for each theme; the content of these datasets was then subjected to secondary coding to extract sub-themes, sub-sub-themes, and beyond, and thematic relationships within and across our focal areas and across our data as a whole. Quotes were organized in the dataset according to the themes, sub-themes, sub-sub-themes, and beyond during the analytical process and refined to ensure all details maintained anonymity and confidentiality (e.g., "[police service redacted]" added) wherever appropriate and necessary.

All research was conducted with approval from the Non-Medical Research Ethics Board (NMREB) at Western University in accordance with the Tri-Council of Canada policies on research ethics.

L. Ferguson, L. Huey, *Police Search and Rescue Response to Lost and Missing Persons*, SpringerBriefs in Criminology,
https://doi.org/10.1007/978-3-031-44077-9

Table A.1 Data included in the book

Dataset	Type	Years	Information
National Policing Study	Interviews and surveys	2019–2022	**Study:** A national study of police responses to lost and missing persons across Canada, involving interviews and surveys with police with professional experience in this work. **Sample**: 61 Interviews and 160 online surveys with police members of varying ranks and positions (civilian and sworn; e.g., law enforcement analysts to frontline patrol to Search Managers to Inspectors to Deputy Chiefs and Chiefs). The total sample is 221 interviews and surveys. Interviews and surveys represent six Canadian provinces: Ontario, British Columbia, Manitoba, Alberta, Nova Scotia, and Saskatchewan, and 42 police services (not identified to ensure confidentiality is maintained). **Guide/Questions:** Interviews utilized a semi-structured interview guide with questions in five main areas: (a) the individual's various roles within their police service, both in the past and in the present; (b) their experiences with lost and missing persons work, when this experience started, and when (if) it concluded and why; (c) the types of cases they typically respond to and the protocols for handling these cases (in their department and individually); (d) the factors that help resolve these cases, including their department's practices, training, and resources and any municipal, provincial, or federal policies or standards; and (e) the challenges they face with these cases, any encountered concerns/criticisms of missing persons work, and how these challenges and concerns should/could be addressed. Surveys contained the same questions as the interview guide, just in an online questionnaire format to improve access to participation (e.g., to attenuate scheduling conflicts and COVID-19 pandemic restrictions). The interviews and surveys, therefore, make up one dataset. **Recruitment:** Participants were selected for interviews and surveys through snowball sampling. This occurred by requesting police involvement through personal social media channels ('X'/Twitter and LinkedIn), reaching out to existing connections in policing and cold-contacting potential respondents through email.

(continued)

Table A.1 (continued)

Dataset	Type	Years	Information
Police Service #1 Records	CAD data	2014–2018	**Dataset:** 65,535 Anonymized calls for police service related to various social- and crime-related incidents, of which our total sample involves 2,543 records linked to lost and missing persons. **Data:** Contains details on reportee and call-taker conversation, and dispatched record. Depicts qualitative and quantitative information on the following: dispatcher/call-taker record; call types; Uniform Crime Reporting (UCR) information; how the call was received; addresses/location; times (received, dispatched, arrived, cleared); incident progress; minutes on call; minutes of response; priority assessment; and disposition.
	RMS data	2014–2018	**Dataset:** 8,519 Anonymized closed (resolved, returned, identified, located, cleared) police missing persons reports. **Data:** Contains details on the lost or missing persons, synopses of all search and investigation activities, case outcomes, and case closure particulars. In essence, it involves all details on the lost or missing persons cases from dispatch to case closure. Depicts qualitative and quantitative information on the following: missing persons information (name [redacted], age and date of birth, sex/gender, race/ethnicity); number of times lost or missing; probable cause; history of going lost or missing; address/location; disability and health information; year missing; time (Place Last Seen (PLS), Place Last Known (PLK), clearance); time to locate; total days and hours missing; place located; urgency classification; harm suffered and caused; and synopsis of occurrence.
	Risk Factor Questionnaires	2014–2018	**Dataset:** Anonymized police risk factor questionnaires completed for 8,914 closed (resolved, returned, identified, located, cleared) missing persons reports. **Data**: Contains risk assessment details for closed cases of lost and missing persons that were updated over the course of the police search and investigation. Depicts qualitative and quantitative information on the following: level of risk assigned; location type; address; lost or missing persons information (Date of birth, race/ethnicity, sex/gender, subject type, age group); probable cause; history of going lost or missing; address missing from; disability and health information; remarks on risk; questionnaire risk factors; search urgency evaluation; and search questionnaire.

(continued)

Table A.1 (continued)

Dataset	Type	Years	Information
Police Service #2 Records	RMS Data	2014–2019	**Dataset:** 2,397 Anonymized closed (resolved, returned, identified, located, cleared) police missing persons reports. **Data:** Contains details on the lost or missing persons, synopses of all search and investigation activities, case outcomes, and case closure particulars. In essence, it involves all details on the lost or missing persons cases from dispatch to case closure. Depicts qualitative and quantitative information on the following: missing persons information (name [redacted], age and date of birth, sex/gender, race/ethnicity); times (occurrence time, response time, closure time); Uniform Crime Reporting status; address/location; probable cause; Place Last Known; medical conditions; date/time located; location found; total days missing; harm sustained and caused; and case summary.

Index

L. Ferguson, L. Huey, *Police Search and Rescue Response to Lost and Missing Persons*, SpringerBriefs in Criminology,
https://doi.org/10.1007/978-3-031-44077-9

MIX
Papier aus verantwortungsvollen Quellen
Paper from responsible sources
FSC® C105338

If you have any concerns about our products,
you can contact us on
ProductSafety@springernature.com

In case Publisher is established outside the EU,
the EU authorized representative is:
Springer Nature Customer Service Center GmbH
Europaplatz 3, 69115 Heidelberg, Germany

Printed by Libri Plureos GmbH
in Hamburg, Germany